INSPIRATION

From Inside

KEEPING THE FAITH WHEN YOUR
FREEDOM IS LIMITED

Daniel J. Pye

Leitourgia Press
COLORADO SPRINGS, COLORADO

Copyright © 2021 by Daniel J. Pye.

All rights reserved. No part of this publication may be reproduced, distributed or transmitted in any form or by any means, including photocopying, recording, or other electronic or mechanical methods, without the prior written permission of the publisher, except in the case of brief quotations embodied in critical reviews and certain other noncommercial uses permitted by copyright law. For permission requests, write to the publisher, addressed "Attention: Permissions Coordinator," at the address below.

Pye/Leitourgia Press
Colorado Springs, CO/80924
www.leitourgiapress.com
Email: info@liturgies.com

Book Layout ©2017 BookDesignTemplates.com

Cover Photo by Danny Pye

Ordering Information:
Quantity sales. Special discounts are available on quantity purchases by corporations, associations, and others. For details, contact the "Special Sales Department" at the address above.

Inspiration from Inside/ Daniel J. Pye. —1st ed.
ISBN 978-0-578-91781-8
Library of Congress Control Number: 2021939270

Contents

Daniel Pye 6

The Power of Pictures 11

East to West: Remember What He's Done 14

Even If 17

God's Not Done With You 20

White as Snow 22

Boundaries 25

Greed 29

If We are the Body 32

Complaining vs Gratitude 35

Be the Light 38

The Cost 41

Deliverance from Despair 45

Rules vs. Relationship 48

Riches versus Love 51

Forgetting 54

The Widow's Plea 57

Witness 60

Mercy of a Stranger 63

Master or Slave	66
Idols	69
Danny's Paintings	72
Account	78
Question	81
Busy	84
Still	87
With Me	90
Pride	93
The Fall	96
Understand	99
Purpose	102
Recycled	105
Condemned	108
Compromise	111
All	114
Meant	117
Neglect	120
Exposed	123
Overcome	126
Preparedness	129

*Dedicated to Leann, Riann, Joseph and Anna Joy
who brought untold joy and hope to me in my
darkest hours*

"It was strictly forbidden to preach to other prisoners. It was understood that whoever was caught doing this received a severe beating. A number of us decided to pay the price for the privilege of preaching, so we accepted their (the communists') terms. It was a deal; we preached and they beat us. We were happy preaching. They were happy beating us, so everyone was happy."

—Richard Wurmbrand, TORTURED FOR CHRIST

ABOUT THE AUTHOR

Daniel Pye

I am a son, a father, a brother, a husband, a teacher, a preacher, a missionary, a student, a patient, a client, an inmate, a friend, a number, a writer, a painter, a reader, an uncle, a cousin, a customer, a helper, a provider, an employee, a citizen, an enemy, an advisor, a mentor.

But more than any of that, I am a forgiven believer, a child of God, redeemed, blameless, and loved. So much has changed in our world. Many more know about seclusion, loneliness and isolation than ever before. So comes this writing from the heart of a prisoner, sharing reflections that have helped me get through. I hope it does the same for you.

Danny Pye

He loved the Haitian children like they were his own and they loved and adored him. Overall, the Haitian people, his friends, staff, neighbors, leaders of the community, everyone loved him and he loved them I saw him work nonstop to do whatever he could to improve the lives of the Haitian people no matter how big or small he was always helping and serving them.

-Jennifer

I have seen Danny in different parts of his life, becoming a husband, becoming a father. I have seen him go through some of the best times and some of the worst times in his life. And I can say he has remained the same hard working, positive, fun loving, caring person he has always been.

-Katie

There was nothing that Danny wouldn't do for those kids. This trait was not limited to the children in his care but to all of the staff, neighbors and complete strangers for that matter. So much so that after the devastating earthquake that Haiti suffered the Mayor put Danny in charge of the small airport in Jacmel and he was the main coordinator of relief efforts in the city until he was relieved by the Canadian Military. I do not believe that Daniel Pye is guilty, nor do I believe that he should be in prison.

-Jon

His compassion and selflessness showed thru this mission trips and the desire to help others. He met and married the love of his life and decided his place was in Haiti to help those unable to help themselves. He raised funds to develop a home for children that had none. He worked unfailingly thru the earthquake, helping organized donations from all over and making sure the people who needed it most got the supplies.

-Alice

I have observed Danny as being a hard-working, family-oriented Christian who constantly thinks of others and how he may be of help to them, sometimes to a fault or detriment to himself and his family, whom he loves very much and who love him and miss his presence.

-David

Danny has worked tirelessly in making sure people were fed and cared for during natural disasters. He has become a father to the fatherless. He continually refuses to burden people with his own struggles and heartbreaks as he knows everyone suffers with their own pain and heartbreak. Danny has always held strongly to his beliefs and refuses to allow his faith to falter. He has always believed in the best of everyone, even those who have done him wrong. Danny and his family have had unmeasurable suffering. He has always been more concerned about others and their suffering, than in his own pain. He has been a light to so many in such a dark angry world. I can only hope that I can be as selfless and dedicated as he has been to so many others. He is my unsung hero.

-Tammy

There is no way to sum up Danny's impact on our lives in a single statement. In the eye of life's storm Danny brought joy, hope, and Christ's love to those around him, even in the darkest places. Danny was a flame where there seemed to be no light. In the smallest of deeds, but the biggest of hearts, Danny magnified hope. We know he has made a permanent imprint on our hearts and continues to offer us a lasting example of life as a gift to others.

-Aaron and Angie

Jesus asks us to lay down our lives for love of Him and that's just what Danny has done, day in and day out, all for the love of Christ. He loved everyone and showed no partiality, even to those who were his enemies. His selflessness and faith are so inspiring.

-Margie

When my trusted friend, Gary, asked me to go with him to Haiti to help the missionary leaders of a non-profit ministry work through their differences, tensions and disagreements, I could not fathom it would take me on the journey that it has these past ten years with Danny Pye. From the outset it was abundantly clear that he was being scapegoated for organizational problems that predictably accompany the growth and development of such a system.

My heart breaks when I witness what well-intentioned Christian people can do to their fellow servants, and I saw the absolute worst of it when Danny was unjustly imprisoned in a Haitian prison that would turn the stomachs of even the vilest among us. It was one of the most rewarding experiences of my life when I was able to accompany a small team who would meet him upon his release (a result of the U.S. Embassy and countless others advocating on his behalf), and usher his frail, broken body to meet his wife and daughter, only hours before Leann would give birth to their son, Joseph.

I assumed this would bring his saga of unjust suffering to an end, but the Judas priests who had manipulated the legal system in Haiti were obviously determined to do Danny harm even to the end...and so they relentlessly found a way to bring the weight of a limitless judicial system down on him. With limited, (almost no), funds to fight the giant of tyranny, Danny took up the only weapon he knew how to wield without fear—truth itself! In one of our many visits during his three-year imprisonment in a Federal prison for crimes he did not commit, I asked him why he would not accept the plea agreement offered him that could have set him free within a few years. His response, of course—"How could I confess to something I didn't do?" It was incredulous for him to even think of denying the truth.

Danny's only crime was in his foolishness...he was a fool for Christ. Such radicals will make the choice to use ministry funds for the family who are starving to death, rather than the new sound system for the church. Such extravagant givers will laugh and embrace the orphan children with crushing bear hugs that would touch them to the core. And such innocents will just assume that a Court of Law will follow the truth, not the lies couched in the words of those with selfish and even evil motivations.

Many of you are like me, or at least like I was before his trial, believing in a judicial system that would always fight for the truth and the rights of all people. That confidence was shattered when I sat in the court room and heard them deliver the conviction of a man who was just trying his foolish best to be a servant of Jesus Christ in the hope that he would one day hear those words, "Well done, good and faithful servant!"

After his wife, other friends, and those present left that austere room where peoples' fates are decided, I remained and watched as he took off his black suit coat, removed his poorly tied tie that never did fit a man like Danny of such humility, and then, when he seemed to be stripped of everything and everyone who meant his life to him, was told to take out his shoestrings. The Sheriff escorted him over to me, where he handed me those laces that now hang from the rearview mirror of my car, fashioned now into a vessel of prayer as a Rosary.

I miss you, my foolish and faithful friend. May we all be so foolish for Christ as to pursue the Truth at all costs!

-Tim

INTRODUCTION

The Power of Pictures

"A picture is worth 1000 words"—or so they say. I moved to a new cell a month or so ago. In this cell there was no mattress, no chair, and no bulletin board. Well, after two weeks, I got a mattress. A week later, a chair, and today a bulletin board. I learned another important tip from a guard who told me "only the squeaky wheel gets oil". From my experience, working with children in education and with my own kids, their persistence in asking for things they wanted annoyed me. My "motto" was— *"the more you ask the less likely you will receive."* I asked for a bulletin board the day I moved into the cell because the rules are you cannot post ANY pictures in your cell unless they are posted on a bulletin board. I almost worked out a trade to "buy" one from a neighbor, but the cheap side of me didn't want to pay for something I should get for free.

Today my bulletin board is full of pictures and happy memories. My wife and kids have done a great job over this past year to take pictures of memorable moments: special hikes, loosing teeth, dentist appointments, braces, concerts, dances, karate matches, bike riding, archery, playing in the snow, playing in the river, happy times and sad times. They have done a great job keeping me involved in this way as to what is going on in their daily lives. It's the best they can do.

I have also stocked up on picture tickets, so as friends and family visit, I can get pictures taken in the visiting arca. Pictures change your environment! They can transform a cold, depressing cell into a home filled with love, care and hope. Going to sleep gazing at my family and loved ones, waking up seeing their beautiful faces, beautiful expressions make another day possible. The bulletin board couldn't have come at a better time. There have been recent fights in the prison, so we have been on "Lock Down" for a week. That means confined to our cell for most of the day as well as the night. It's all about the small things. That's what really matters when it is all said and done. Just a simple picture.

ESCAPE

I will have to watch what I say or how I word these blogs that I'm writing inside prison. I thought I was alone, and maybe a little crazy, but I learned I am not alone, (I might still be crazy).

I learned this when my wife's Aunt requested, I paint a landscape of her "happy place". I found that wording kind of ironic. I realize this is one of the many reasons I paint every day. Whether at the recreation center or in my cell, I paint to escape the walls of prison. I paint to escape myself, my negativity, my environment. I paint to escape the sights and smells and the noise of prison. I often imagine myself to be in the location of what I am painting. You will see a common theme in my paintings: sunsets, sunrises, the glowing light of the moon, in the country, camping, the ocean, trees, anywhere outside is where I long to be. I like to use lots of color you'll see. I am reminded daily that I have to deal with my emotions and conquer the frequent bouts of depression. Escaping now and then, taking a journey in my imagination, is a fun distraction that lasts a moment or sometimes even hours. It helps to give me the courage and energy to forge through the less than pleasant experiences of prison.

CHAPTER ONE

East to West: Remember What He's Done

Tribute to Riann
Father's Day 2020

While being incarcerated, one of the good and bad things is you have endless time to think. The time is endless to reflect, to remember, to relive the life I once lived. I have been married for eighteen years now. As I look back to my past, as I reflect, I find myself so critical of my many mistakes, and of the many things I have done and said to hurt my wife and my children. Things I see now as so small and not worth the effort of thought, less an argument. I am sad at the time I wasted, the time I took for granted. Often this leads me to feelings of guilt and shame, and feelings of being worthless.

I ask for forgiveness, but there is no turning back time to undo the hurts and to take back harsh words. In the same way, I don't fully receive the forgiveness from God when I don't forgive myself or others for the wrongs I have done, or the wrongs done to me. It is hard to receive and to fully understand God's forgiveness, to understand His grace and mercy. I hope this helps your own understanding, your own growth as it is in fact, helping mine.

This lesson was taught to me this month by my 14-year-old daughter as she opened up with me on the phone on Father's Day. She shared her struggle to forgive those that have hurt her and those that have lied. Her Youth Pastor spoke and taught about the concept of "if we want God to forgive us for all of our sins, we must in turn forgive those that have hurt us". My daughter wrestled with this idea so much that it brought her to tears. She felt confused, angry, and sad. She asked her Pastor and God how she could forgive those that have hurt her so badly by ripping her family apart and taking her father away? She shared this with me later on that evening on a monitored call. What a privilege it was to talk with my daughter about the importance of forgiveness. I shared how it frees us more than anything else we can do. I encouraged her to "let go and let God"-let him justly fix the wrong that was done. What a privilege to have that conversation with my daughter. How mature of her to wrestle with the idea of forgiveness and to see the need to forgive and have the desire to forgive.

She feels so betrayed. I am so proud of her and happy to know she shared her heart with the Pastor's wife, and with her mom, and then me. My eyes filled with tears as my heart was so grateful that my daughter, at her young age, chooses to wrestle with real life challenges. I am so proud to watch her growth, both physically and spiritually. She, by her example, shows me the importance of forgiveness. Then I reflect on His forgiveness of me, and my many sins.

Read **Psalm 103**

Two songs come to my mind as I write these words. The first is a beautiful song by Casting Crowns, ***East to West***, in which I am reminded what God has done to my own sins, having cast them as far as the east is from the west. The other song is ***Forgiveness*** by Matthew West where he says it so powerfully, ***"It's the opposite of how you feel when the pain they caused is just too real, takes everything you have to say the word...forgiveness, forgiveness."***

> *Father God,*
>
> *Teach me to forgive as you have forgiven me. Teach me to love the unlovable. Teach me to reach the unreachable. Father God, help me to see people as you see them. Father God, help me to forgive those that have hurt me so! Father God, help me to show your love, your grace, your mercy, and your forgiveness to the men that surround me today.*
>
> *In your name I pray,*
>
> *Amen*

CHAPTER TWO

Even If

July 2020

Today's message is one of the most powerful messages, but one that I personally don't like to consider. I relate to Paul in his words found in 1 Corinthians 9:19-27, as he strives to seek to understand. My heart aches for all of those leaders, all the pastors and teachers that share the good news day and night, tirelessly. They preach and teach the faith by word and by action. Yet, when their own faith is tested, when those that serve and give everything are put through trials and temptations, when they face the fire, who then is there to support them, to lift them up, to pray for them, to encourage them?

Then he goes on to ask that hard, age-old question—What if God does not answer your prayer? What if God says "No", or "Wait" or is just silent? Why do bad things happen to good people? Why are God's servants not protected? Why aren't they saved from illness and affliction? What if God does not answer your prayer request the way you want or expect? Is He still the same God? When He says "No", or "Wait"? Is He still faithful? Is God still good?

One of my favorite Biblical examples of this is found in the third chapter of Daniel, when the king confronts the three men that followed God's laws by not worshipping an idol. Shadrach, Meshach and Abednego said one of the most profound statements in verse 18 when they were confronted with the death sentence if they were not obedient to the king's law. They knew the God they served could save them from the fire, but *even if* their God didn't save them, they still would not compromise God's law. Wow!

In Matthew 17:21, it is written, "If you have faith as small as a mustard seed, it is enough. You can say to this mountain 'Move from here to there', and it will move. Nothing will be impossible for you." But what if God chooses not to move the mountain.

One of my favorite Christian groups, **Mercy Me**, has a song that puts it so remarkably, **Even If**. Consider this line from the song—"I know the sorrow I know the hurt, would all go away if you just say the word. But even if you don't, my hope is you alone."

Read *Psalm 104*

Father God,

Help me to accept your plan for me today. Help me to see the good you do, the good you are. When life does not meet my expectations, or my hopes, let me rest in knowing you are a good God. Help me to rest in knowing that it is well with my soul. Help me to see that today. Help me to believe that today. Help me to share that same love and grace with the men I am surrounded by today.

In Your Name,

Amen

CHAPTER THREE

God's Not Done With You

July 2020

For days, weeks, months, and years now I have wrestled with God in my prayers and devotion. I have self-righteously listed all I have done in my lifetime for Christ, and I begged in agony that it was enough, that I've given enough of myself, and the sacrifice was sufficient, that I could be in fact be done here on earth and transcend to eternity with my Father in heaven. I have made countless attempts to end my own life, which only made me more miserable, in more pain and still present in mind and body on this earth. If it sounds like I am feeling sorry for myself, let me admit that I am in fact. I believe it was okay after all I have done to feel finished, to be finished and when it became evident over and over again that I was not yet done, I drowned myself in self-pity, believing that "Woe is me".

Today as I pray, as I read His word and worship in song, I am reminded that God's not done with me yet. I am faced with a choice. I can fight God and continue my self -destructive behavior, or I can submit and cry out for His mercy and grace to be new every morning. I can pray that I will not only fulfill His calling on my life, but that I will do so with a contrite and joyful spirit. I pray that I will love as He loves and that I will give as He gives, serve as He serves, while I am here on earth and while I am in prison.

I am reminded in Philippians 1:6 *"God began a good work in you and I am sure that he will carry it on until it is completed."* That will be on the day Christ Jesus returns!

Read *Psalm 6*

Tarren Wells, in his song **God's Not Done with You**, reminds all of us that "He's got a plan. This is part of it. He's going to finish what He started."

> *Father God,*
>
> *Help me to accept that You are not done with me yet. Help me to embrace your calling on my life today, tomorrow and forever. Help me to love as you love, to serve as you serve to give as you give in here in prison. God, may I do it with a contrite heart and joyful heart.*
>
> *In Your Name,*
>
> *Amen*

CHAPTER FOUR

White as Snow

"*Come, let us settle this matter,' says the Lord. 'Even though your sins are bright red, they will be as white as snow. Even though they are deep red, they will be white like wool.'*" (Isaiah 1:18)

The longer that I am incarcerated, the more I enjoy working with my hands in art and crafts. Many of you know that I love painting. Another hobby I have is working with leather. Something I learned early on is that most mistakes are easy to fix, easy to go over and correct.

One exception, however, I have found is when working with the color red. A deep red pigment is the hardest to cover. It's the hardest to blend and the most challenging to change, remove or erase. I see this especially in oil painting. I make it look more like mud as I try to change the color red into something else. I also found this true when working in dye with leather. Once I commit to a deep red and I begin treating and dying my leather, there is no going back. I can't undo what I've done, especially with red. It's impossible to hide or cover or change. Red is, to be certain, a very strong color or stain.

Well, as we get closer to Christmas, I am again reminded of this simple lesson. My current cellmate is very artistic. He enjoys crafts even more than I do and he's more creative. We decided to make Christmas Stockings for each other and for our friends, out of old holy socks which I had plenty of. We also made a Christmas tree and a Christmas hat to wear. This was all out of rags and old socks. My cellmate did the hours of sewing and creating. My job was to use my leather dyes that I had in my cell to decorate the items. Since in lockdown, I had no way to use the dyes on real leather, so this was a good outlet.

We made a pretty good team and the many projects turned out really well. I was amazed at seeing the transformation of old socks with holes into new, colorful, creative objects. I learned that brushing the dyes was better than dipping into them. I spent days trying to get the colors off my hands and clothes. The hardest color to clean off was, you guessed it, red.

So, as I reflect on the deep reading today in Isaiah and the marvelous miracle God did to change red to white, pure white, I know something of what a big deal that is. To have no trace of red is an impossible task. I couldn't imagine changing something scarlet red to something snow white. Yet, God can do this in a moment. He forgives my sins and removes them as far away as the East is from the West. He leaves no blemish. There is no trace of it. There is no evidence, no smell, no dot, nothing! He is amazing! Supernatural! Almost impossible to comprehend! And he does it all through his Son, Jesus Christ.

Father God,

Thank you for your forgiveness! Thank you for your redemption. Thank you for erasing my sins, my faults, my bad habits, my misdeeds, all that I have done or said that has hurt so many, that has hurt you. You have forgiven me for all of it. You have no record of my sins any longer. Your grace has covered me. The stain of your blood on the cross has set me free from death, from eternal separation. Thank you for washing me clean. Thank you for making me a sinner called righteous in you! Thank you for the cross. Help me to live my life in freedom by your grace and no longer be shamed by my sin.

In your name I pray,

Amen.

CHAPTER FIVE

Boundaries

We see them in every aspect of our life, boundaries. They aren't bad, in fact, they are often there for our own good, for our safety. For example, boundaries are put in place in sporting events to help with safety and the competition. You can see it in every sport: volleyball, football, basketball, soccer, hockey, swimming, track, golf, tennis, and the list goes on. Can you imagine if there were no boundaries set ahead of time?

Soccer players could dribble the ball anywhere and everywhere to avoid their opponent before scoring a goal. It would be complete chaos. The competition would be far less.

The same is true in travel. If our roads weren't clearly marked for travel in one direction, or sides clearly marked and barriers put up, we would see all kinds of accidents. People would go the wrong way and drive off the side of the road and even off mountains or cliffs or into water. Again, there would be chaos. We have clear boundaries set up in school, work, even in our relationships. All for the purpose of protection and to create and maintain order. They are a necessity.

We see this same thing in the beginning of humankind. We see boundaries set up in the Garden of Eden. I was taught as a child about our God who had rules. There were things I could do and things I could not do. As I reflect, and read His Word today, and as I pray, I see God, not as the God that says "no". I don't see Him as a God of restriction and rules. "He came to give us life, and life abundantly." We have freedom in Him. True Freedom. There are so many more *dos'* than *don'ts*.

I'd like to share a short Scripture that will hopefully help you to see Him in the same way. It is not only the truth, but it is the more constructive, helpful way to see Him.

"The Lord God gave the man a command. He said, "You may eat fruit from any tree in the garden, but you must not eat the fruit from the tree of knowledge of good and evil. If you do, you will certainly die" (Genesis 2: 16-17).

The simple reality is the Garden of Eden was full of different fruit bearing trees, and other plants. Adam and Eve had plenty of choices and they would have never lacked for good, nutritious food. God said you can eat it all! Then God gave them a boundary. It was a very small boundary, limiting them from eating of only one tree. Why did God do that? Was He really not wanting Adam and Eve to have His best creation? Was He punishing them? No. He didn't want them to die. He didn't want them to be separated from Him. Up to this point in the story, Adam and Eve communed with God daily. They had no shame despite their nakedness. They were *free*. God wanted the best for them. He didn't want to restrict them. He wanted them to enjoy the freedom of choosing from all of His wonderful creations.

As I reflect on this Scripture today, I ask myself how I'm doing with accepting the boundaries in my own life. Do I see them as necessary? Am I thankful for them? Do I realize the freedoms that I do enjoy, or do I just resent the boundaries and feel restricted by them? Do I wish they weren't there? Do I wish for more freedom?

I want to live a life of contentment inside my boundaries.

> *Father God,*
>
> *Thank you for the freedom I have. I lack for nothing even inside these walls. Help me to always see the boundaries that are in my life as your protection. Help me to always be grateful for the boundaries you put in my life.*
>
> *In Your Name I pray!*
>
> *Amen*

CHAPTER SIX

Greed

Idle time...I have so much of it. Day and night, minute to minute, hour to hour, week to week. Idle time is something that seems almost endlessly available to me, with very few responsibilities and the constant lock down in a very small cell. I am left to my own thoughts, my own reflections, and my own imagination.

I'm struggling today. During my quiet time, I ask God in one of my rather odd prayers and I suspect many can relate. The deepest wound that I suffer from, that hurts worse than any other is the betrayal. Sure, as a family member or a spouse, I can truly be caught in this snare easily. But this wound comes from a fellow believer, from a friend, from a confidante. To me there is nothing that hurts more than a deep betrayal from a friend, a brother in Christ. I seek God today to find the cause, the reason that my friend betrayed me.

I find a simple answer to be this—the person was not really a friend. Maybe not even a Christian believer. What if you were in my shoes and thought the individual was a true friend? This is the answer I believe God gave to me when I asked him this question:

"Watch out, be on your guard against wanting to have more and more things. Life is not made up of how much a person has" (Luke 12:16).

"We didn't bring anything into the world. We can't take anything out of it" (1 Timothy 6:7).

Paul summarized it the best when he said, *"The love of money is the root of all evil"* (1 Timothy 6:10).

The evil is not in having money, nor in the fact that you are wise in your money. There is no fault or shame in this. But backing up to Luke 12, we are reminded that when God blesses you, what is your response? Do you build a bigger building to hold the extra blessing? Or do you bless others with the plenty you have been given? What kind of steward or manager are you? If you can't be trusted with the little you have, why do you beg and plead with God to give you more? First, show that you are a generous, loving, compassionate steward with the little you've been entrusted with. Then, God will give you more.

When I want, when I take something that never belonged to me in the first place, God does not bless that. God does not allow you to keep that. Are you surprised? Are you angry? The blessings come from God and Him alone. It does not come from our greed. It does not come from our entitled attitudes or our demands for more.

If you struggle with greed from day to day. If you find you struggle with never having enough, try the opposite. Start being grateful for what you have. Do that in your actions and in your words. Pray daily thanking God for taking care of you. List the small victories. Be generous. Give to your church. Give to a neighbor in need. Don't just give money, but also give your time and energy and talents. Be an example for others, especially your children. Let them hear how grateful you are. You have the power to change your mindset, your attitude, and ultimately your entire lifestyle and even your situation by changing your perspective. God will entrust you with more when he sees you're being faithful. Why do you hold so tight to things that disappear? It is all His.

Father God

Change my attitude. Change my perspective. Help me to see all you have blessed me with and to thank you for it. Help me not to take something that is not mine. Help me to see you in everything.

In your name I pray,

Amen

CHAPTER SEVEN

If We are the Body

"But if we are the Body, why aren't His arms reaching? Why aren't His hands healing? Why aren't His words teaching? And if we are the Body, why aren't His feet going? Why is His love not showing them there is a way, there is a way!" Those words are taken from another of the repertoire of songs by the group, **Casting Crowns**.

Jesus paid much too high a price, for us to pick and choose who should come. And we are the Body of Christ. Jesus is the Way! The message is simple. We are the Body, don't leave it up to your Pastor, or Priest. Don't leave it to the institution of the church. Be the Church. You might be the only Christ, the only church that someone meets, that someone knows, that someone works with. We are all essential to the body, we all have a purpose, and God has a plan for each of us.

My Scripture reading today is from 1 Corinthians 12: 12-31. I would encourage you to read the entire passage. "There is one body, but it has many parts. But all its parts make up one body. It is the same with Christ. We are all baptized by one Holy Spirit. And so, we are formed into one body..." and it gets even better as it goes on, so please read it.

I think of the deep hurt that my wife and I experienced at one church. I remember the hurt that our kids felt. We were rejected. Being judged is never pleasant. For me today, I want to stop and evaluate my own actions and words that I have expressed to others that have hurt them. I remember today that I am part of the Body of Christ, so when I judge, when I reject others, what are they seeing in me? How do they view Christ and His love, His mercy, His forgiveness? When I represent Christ, when I am part of the Body of Christ, am I hurtful? I maybe the only Christ that a person sees. What does he see? Obviously, I will never be perfect. I will never be without sin. But I can still live my life in a way that accepts those that Christ brings my way. I can show them mercy, His mercy. This is the same gift of forgiveness that I have been given.

Father God,

Help me to be your hands and feet today and every day. Help those that see me to see you in me. Help me never to push people away by my own narrow views. Help me to love as you love me. Help me to be humble when I make mistakes. Help me to be quick to make them right. Help those that know me to want to know more about You because of the love I show them. Help me to be inclusive and never excluding. Help me to be welcoming and accepting of others you put in my path. I thank you for the body of Christ, and for the countless times I was loved and encouraged by others. Help me to do the same.

In your name Jesus I pray,

Amen.

CHAPTER EIGHT

Complaining vs Gratitude

December 2020

As I take time to reflect today, I believe a lot of my hardships and struggles, a lot of my depression and anxiety are due to the fact that I have spent much of my life complaining. I have said I have reason to complain because of significant loss and trials and injustice. I have excused my behavior and in doing so, I have only hurt myself more. I have missed out on countless blessings from the Lord. I created a distance between me and Christ. I have failed to see His provisions, time and time again. This has hurt my relationship with Christ. This has hurt my relationship with my family and friends. This has hurt my testimony and my ability to help others.

The best example of this is found in the Scripture in the story of Moses and the Israelites when they were in the wilderness for forty years. The story begins in Exodus with the Israelites enslaved to the Egyptians. God called Moses to rise up and set them free from slavery. Moses, with the help of his brother, Aaron, pleaded and negotiated with Pharaoh to let the Israelites go free. God provided signs and miracles and even plaques to try to convince Pharaoh to let them go. Even after Pharaoh agreed out of his desperation, he changed his mind. He pursued the Israelites as they were fleeing to recapture them.

God showed up again, and swept Pharaoh's army into the Red Sea, and allowed the Israelites to walk across on dry land to freedom. The Israelites saw how God protected them and guided them by a cloud during the day and fire in the sky at night. God provided food for them in the desert. God provided fresh water for them from a rock. He caused their shoes and clothes to last and not be worn out. All of their needs were met. Despite all God did, the Israelites grumbled and complained against God and Moses their leader. They complained about their food and provisions. They wanted something different. They forgot how bad it was being slaves and how God had redeemed them. They even said it would have been better to be left enslaved in Egypt.

I reflect on this story and am enraged at their ungratefulness. How could they miss *** all*** that God did for them?! I can't imagine how this made God feel. I can't imagine how this made Moses feel to hear all of the negativity and complaining, despite God's provisions and Moses's efforts. How heartbreaking and how sad. But then it hits me. Haven't I done the same as the Israelites? I have never gone a whole day without food or water. My clothes and shoes have never worn out to the point of being totally useless. Yet how often do I complain?! How often am I ungrateful?! How often am I blinded by my own perceived misery? How often do I miss God's faithful hand that leads me and provides for me?! The sad truth is...***too often***.

But I resolve to change that today. From now on, I will start my days listing the ***many*** things that I am grateful for. I will write daily in my gratitude journal. When times get harder, when the pandemic hits, and lock downs are extended and I have no access to family and friends during the holidays, I will still find my list of gratitude growing longer and longer despite my circumstances. I will still look for and see God's provisions.

Father God,

Help me to always see your provisions. Help me to always see your grace. Help me to be grateful in all things. Help me to spread that around so that others my see my gratitude and want to know where that attitude came from. Help me to be able to share effectively

In your name,

Amen.

CHAPTER NINE

Be the Light

December 2020

Living in a developing country, a fourth world country like Haiti for over a decade, I witnessed some of nature's most beautiful creations. Yet, because of the poverty and desolation of the country, I also witnessed the *power of light*. When electricity doesn't exist and isn't even available for some fourteen hours out of the day, and even those few hours it might be available aren't a guarantee, given faulty wiring, old and used transformers, limited fuel, and other issues with generators—light is a luxury! Electricity is expensive, so it is not available to everyone. In fact, it's not available to most people.

Some of my favorite memories in Haiti were made while driving down the mountains that separated the North Peninsula,

Leggone from the Southern Peninsula, Jacmel. We could see our Children's Home from miles and miles away when the sky was clear. We could recognize businesses and other homes that were lit up in the pitch back night. Another memory was the evening walks we would take on the beach. It was so dark without lights and also so quiet. We loved to look at the beautiful clear sky, filled with stars, full of wonders that God created. Another favorite memory comes back to me from our first year in Haiti when we lived on top of a mountain in the village of Sequin. There was no electricity at all there. At night, we'd see some candles lighting up huts. Our home was run on a generator when it worked. Again, you could see our home from thousands of feet away, even miles and miles away. I was always amazed at how far just a little light could travel in pitch darkness.

Read **Psalm 18**

> ***"People do not light a lamp and put it under a bowl. Instead, they put it on its stand. Then it gives light to everyone in the house. In the same way, let your light shine so others can see it. Then they will see the good things you do, and they will glorify your Father, who is in heaven" (Matthew 5: 15-16).***

> ***"The light shines in the darkness, but the darkness has not overcome the light" (John 1:5).***

I am beginning to recognize how dark of a place I live in -this Federal Penitentiary. I see the need for light, hope, and grace. I know that by sharing the Gospel of Christ, both through words and actions, I am bringing the light into this dark place. But this message is not just for me. In this time of the COVID pandemic, when our country is so divided, this message of light and hope in Christ is one everyone needs to hear and take to heart. I hope all of us can take the time to discover the difference we can make by just shining some of Christ's light that lives within us.

> *Father God,*
>
> *I can't do it on my own. But you can shine your light in me and through me. Help me to shine your light in this dark place so those around me will see and hear the good news of your grace and love. Help my words and my actions to share your mercies. Father, God, use me today as you will.*
>
> *In your name,*
>
> *Amen.*

CHAPTER TEN

The Cost

"Faith means trusting God for everything, even when we can't make sense out of anything" (Anonymous).

A Christian song has a powerful line in it—"What if I give all I have? What will that gift do?" And in response, "My child, a gift like that can change the world, it could free a multitude" (Shepherd Boy).

I reflect on that song as I consider the cost of my imprisonment. Everything has a cost. The cost to incarcerate a Federal inmate like me is estimated to be $76,000 per year. But in actuality the cost is so much greater. Take me—a taxpayer, away from my family as the primary financial contributor and all that has cost my family over the years. I have spent many hours dwelling on those facts, saddened by the facts and sometimes angered at them. But today as I reflect, I am humbled by a new and completely different outlook. The truth is God wants *all* of us, not just a part. He wants us to sacrificially give everything to Him. I just read in Scripture, *"...many rich people threw large amounts into them"* (referring to the offering boxes), *"but a poor widow came and put in two very small copper coins, worth only a few pennies..."*. Jesus said, *"The poor widow has put more into the offering box then all the others. They gave a lot because they are rich. But she gave even though she is poor. She put in everything she had, all that she had to live on"* (Mark 12: 41-43).

The impact that this story has had over the years and still has on us today is more powerful than anything money can buy. Because, to the Temple, her offering meant nothing. To the widow, her offering meant everything. But even more important than any of those perspectives is that to God, her sacrifice *"freed a multitude."* Her message, her heart, her sacrifice is taught all around the world and makes an impact on the giving of those that hear it.

The Scripture never mentions if she became suddenly rich by being blessed in some mysterious way for her sacrifice. Jesus is never referenced as publicly recognizing this woman of faith for her amazing sacrifice. She may not have gained anything here on earth for her sacrificial giving. However, we learn that it made an eternal difference. It still is making an eternal difference today. It is making a difference in me.

"Suppose I give everything I have to the poor, and suppose I give myself over to a difficult life so that I can brag about my sacrifices. If I don't have love, I get nothing at all" (1 Corinthians 13:3).

It's not about who you are, it's about what you gave. It's not about what you've done, it's not about where you've been. It's about your heart. It's about your sacrifice. It's about your love. It's about your obedience. It's about your humility. It's about your willingness.

As I stop and consider the cost of ministering to the poor in Haiti, I recall the good I was able to do there. I remember all I gave, and all I gave up. That brings me to focusing on all I lost. It cost me **everything**!

Then I realize that God doesn't see it that way. Therefore, I shouldn't look at it that way either. If just one person was changed because of learning about Christ's love, then the cost was worth it. ***The redemption of one soul is worth all of it!***
God has shown me over and over again that what I have done for His kingdom will always outweigh the cost. The ministry continues in Haiti today. Lives are still being changed. People are being saved. It will never compare to the cost. My cost is **nothing** compared to what God is using for His glory and honor. I end with remembering the cost that Jesus came to earth to pay for the forgiveness of my sins. It cost him the cross. That was the ultimate cost. Jesus says, we are worth it. He says that I am worth it.

Father God,

When I am feeling down with despair, help me to remember the sacrifice you made for me. Help me to remember that your sacrifice was far greater than any sacrifice I have or will experience. Thank you for the gift of life! Thank you for accepting the cost for me and suffering the cross for me. Help me to continue to see the life you have given me the freedom to live even here.

In Jesus' name,

Amen

CHAPTER ELEVEN

Deliverance from Despair

I don't believe that deliverance is a ***one-and-done*** thing. In fact, I don't think that is true with most of the things in our faith journey. Forgiveness, Love, Trust, Joy, Happiness, Peace, Faith, Contentment, Hope, the list goes on. I don't think any of those are one and done. I think that is what Christ is talking about when He instructs us to "work out our salvation." All these attributes take time, practice. Each takes the effort of making a decision to live them out each day in our lives. Each requires work.

I really do believe God has delivered me from despair. It doesn't mean I don't ever experience despair, or that I won't ever experience it again in the future. I believe I have a mental illness. I have suffered from this most of my life. Depression or feelings of despair can come upon me and overwhelm me sometimes without a preceding incident or crisis. So it is something I will struggle with for the rest of my life. Yet, I believe God has delivered me from despair because I know He has provided a *way out*. He is the *way*!

I have learned more and more as I learn to rely on Him. As I have learned to cry out to Him for deliverance, I have found He will *always* give me a way out. He may never open the prison doors and make me a *free* man, but I am learning to live in deliverance inside of these walls.

I think this is one of the most important lessons in my life and I hope and pray it can help someone else someday. There is no quick answer or a magic button that frees me from my despair. I spend time each day in God's word. I read devotionals every day. Every day I write in my journal. I list things that I am grateful for that day. I focus on the positive. I listen to others' stories and as I do, God reveals to me how blessed I am.

Even in my prison cell my door is filled with inspirational quotes from famous Christians, Pastors, and authors. If I read something that speaks to me, I cut it out and put a dab of toothpaste on it to make it stick. I have pictures on my walls of the paintings I have painted. I have Bible verses posted all over my cell along with letters and cards that I have received. My bulletin board is full of pictures of those I love and cherish. I keep a calendar that keeps me grounded in the moment and helps me to look ahead to anything and everything I can look forward to experiencing. It helps me not to dwell on the past. I keep my days busy with letter writing, blog writing and some writing on my book. I spend a lot of time in prayer.

I wake up in the morning and read out of my two devotional books and spend time reading my Bible. Throughout my day I listen to Christian radio. I have three options locally. I also have an MP3 player that has at this point 170 Christian songs on it. I surround myself with good Christian men who try as I do to honor and glorify God in their actions and words. I am quick to be kind to my neighbor and quick to talk to anyone that wants some conversation. I try to greet everyone with a friendly smile and a sincere question of their well-being.

I distract myself with jokes and banter. I play cards and other games with my peers. I take time to exercise. I try to take care of my body the best I am able. I eat three meals a day and try to share with those who have less than I have. I end my days listening to inspiring stories and messages on the Christian talk radio. I go to sleep each night after saying my prayers, listening to my MP3 player's music which I put on a timer. It really helps me to fall asleep listening to worship music. I'm *far* from perfect, but these are the behaviors that I am intent about doing that give me a ***way out*** from despair.

Thank you, Lord!

In Jesus Name,

Amen

CHAPTER TWELVE

Rules vs. Relationship

As I have aged, my relationship with my parents has changed. At one time I used to resent my parents' discipline, but as an adult I see it completely different as now I try my best to raise my own children. My father has become one of my closest friends and supporters over the years. As I reflect upon my relationship with my Heavenly Father I see much in the form of similarities. ***"When I was a child, I acted like a child. I reasoned like a child, but when I became a man",*** I needed that firm hand of guidance. I needed the rules clearly laid out along with the consequences enforced justly. The same guidance was needed when I was a young Christian. Now that I'm grown, I know I still can go to my Dad for advice. Yet, I also see that the instruction he instilled in me over the years has already taught me much of what I needed to know.

As a child, my view of God was an authoritarian king sitting on his throne, dictating rules. He seemed to just take all the fun away from life. It seemed God limited our freedom and forced us to live boring lives compared to those that lived in the world. My Christian faith was built upon rules and roles, what to do and what not to do. What to listen to and what not to listen to? Where to go and who to talk to and where not to go and who to avoid. I was taught how to dress, speak, act and the list seemed endless. As I look back now, I realize how much I resented the rules. I even resented the Scripture I was told to memorize. But now I see it all differently. The life I was taught and the Scripture I learned gave me the foundation that I needed later in my life as I led our ministry and family.

Today, as I study the Scriptures a new, I see things completely different. My perspective has changed. I no longer see God as a dictator trying to limit my freedom. I no longer see God as a God of rules. I realize that God wants to have a relationship with me. He longs to be my Father and my best friend. He longs to comfort me in my despair, to laugh with me in my joy, and to celebrate with me in my victories and to help me learn from my failures. God is here with me in the highest of highs and the lowest of lows. Nothing I do can change God's love for me. His love is not conditional, as I used to imagine.

Rules exist because of our relationship. God loves us so much that He doesn't want us to be hurt. He doesn't want us to be lost from Him. He cares so much for us that He doesn't want us, *any* of us, no matter what we've done, to die and spend eternity in hell. The evidence of His great love for us is that He gave His one and only Son to live a life of hell on this earth as he was mistreated, abandoned, betrayed, and suffered a humiliating death, a criminal's death on the cross. He did that to save us because He loves us.

Accept His love, accept His grace.

Now I follow the rules God left for me because of my love for Him. This is where I find true freedom.

> *Father God,*
>
> *Help me to see you as you truly are—my Friend, my Father, my God. Help me to share the love you have with all the men I am surrounded by. Help me to share your grace and mercy with them in spite of or despite who they have been and what they have done.*
>
> *In Your Name I Pray,*
>
> *Amen*

CHAPTER THIRTEEN

Riches versus Love

"Give and it will be given to you. A good amount will be poured into your lap. It will be pressed down, shaken together, and running over. The same amount you give will be measured out to you." (Luke 6:38)

Growing up in a Christian family and attending church most of my life, I am familiar with so many Scriptures in the Bible. This one specifically has been used in so many sermons. Most of them have the theme of *tithing*, giving generously to the Lord's work. Yet, as I read and pray today, I see this in a totally different context than I have understood it over the years.

When reading Scripture, it is easy to take individual verses or segments of the Word and twist them to apply to a specific topic or purpose, to try to prove the point you are trying to make. However, it is important to read the verses before and after the specific verse you are using to better understand what is being taught.

I would encourage you to read all of chapter 6 in Luke, but I'll share a few more verses to explain.

Starting at verse 27-35, *"Here is what I tell you who are listening. Love your enemies. Do good to those who hurt you. Bless those who call down curses on you. Pray for those who treat you badly. Do to others as you want them to do to you. Suppose you love those who love you. Should anyone praise you for that? Even sinners love those who love them. But love your enemies. Do good to them. Lend to them without expecting to get anything back. Then you will receive a lot in return. You will be children of the Most High God. He is kind to people who are evil and are not thankful."*

God is so much more concerned with our relationships than He is with our wealth. He wants us to love each other, those we consider to be friends, as well as those we consider to be enemies. We are to love everyone all of the time...regardless.

I believe God is talking about blessings because of the way we give our love, our time, and our talents. When we invest ourselves in another person the blessings will come. This is my interpretation of the Scriptures I shared from Luke 6 and how I see them to hold true in my life.

I have seen first-hand how impoverished people give generously to the church and yet never gain riches. However, the Lord took care of their needs. They also were rich in relationships. This has also happened in my own life. I have been rewarded after investing myself in loving my neighbors. When I love those who are difficult to love, God has blessed me time and time again with friendships that were unexpected. I also have been blessed by people caring for me when I didn't deserve it.

At the same time, how do we view the value of our friendships or relationships? God also teaches us in these verses that the value of a friend is more precious than gold or silver. God wants us to see life from a different perspective. Too often we are so busy pursuing wealth that we forget what is most important. We forsake the time needed to spend with our family members. Too often we are so busy running the *rat race* of life, that we miss the opportunity to invest ourselves in our churches, schools or community.

Father God,

Help me to see people as you do. Help me to nurture my friendships and value my relationships over wealth and comfort. Help me to be intentional about building people up and seeing the real value in them.

In Jesus' Name,

Amen

CHAPTER FOURTEEN

Forgetting

"If I forget what is behind me. I push hard toward what is ahead of me." (Philippians 3:13)

Stop focusing on your past and look towards your future with hope and anticipation.

I think this message is even more important as I look back over the year 2020. What I think of as I consider forgetting is to be purposeful in letting go. Often, we hold on too tightly to our past offenses. We harbor memories that turn into bitterness.

The biggest stumbling block that not forgetting causes is unforgiveness. Unforgiveness can cripple us. Forgetting is not the act of erasing a hurt as if it was never there, it is letting go of the pain it causes.

Too often many of us have been the *victim*. We have been wounded by an individual, a group, an organization, a workplace, a church, or a school. Some of us have been wounded many times by many different people, places and events.

I am one of those persons. I dream about the people who have hurt me. I relive the events in my head. For me, nothing constructive comes from the time and attention I spend doing that. Yes, we can learn from our past, and should. However, for me, I'm past the learning stage. I live with regret and that can often turn to anger and bitterness which leads to resentment. That is the power I often give my past. But not anymore! At least that is my resolution for 2021. I resolve to forget and let go of my past hurts and those who caused them. Even though I still feel the scars and still feel the effects, I choose not to dwell on what happened. For me, I choose to leave it all in the arms of Christ. He paid my debt, so he can also take care of the baggage I carry. I choose to *let go*.

But then, what's next? I must replace this behavior. Letting go is not a *one-and-done* action. Sometimes I have to do it many times throughout the day when the memories arise.

So, to meet the goal of *looking ahead* as the Scripture and my quotes state, I will focus on what lies ahead, and make every effort to do my best each day. I will let go of remembering the mistakes of yesterday. I will embrace the present and look with anticipation toward tomorrow. I will be hopeful, believing brighter days are yet to come. I will extend the same grace to others that has been extended to me.

Father God,

Help me to "let go" of my past hurts and wounds. Help me to walk forward proudly with my scars with hope and anticipation of a better tomorrow. Thank you for being my God of today. Thank you for being my God of redemption and forgiveness.

In Your Name I Pray,

Amen.

CHAPTER FIFTEEN

The Widow's Plea

Jesus told his disciples a story. He wanted to show them that they should always pray and not give up. He said,
"In a certain town, there was a judge. He didn't have any respect for God or care about what people thought. A widow lived in that town. She came to the judge again and again. She begged him to make things right for her because someone was treating her badly. The judge refused. But finally, he said to himself, 'I don't have any respect for God or care what others think, but this widow keeps bothering me. I will see that things are made right for her, If I don't, she may someday come and attack me."
(Luke 18: 1-5)

I reflect today on my own prayer life. Although I feel that it has improved over the years, I wonder if I have ever been as determined and as persistent as this widow? More often the not, I am guilty of asking once, twice, maybe even three times, yet then decide that God doesn't care, or He's too busy, if I don't get an answer. Or I think that maybe His answer is "No". I don't like to be annoying. Listen to the end of the story.

"The Lord said, 'Listen to what the unfair judge says. God's chosen people cry out to him day and night. Won't He make things right for them? Will He keep putting them off? I tell you; God will see that things are made right for them. He will make sure it happens quickly. But, when the Son of Man comes, will He find people on earth who have faith?"

Do I have faith in my loving God that He cares enough about me to answer my prayers? Why do I give up so quickly then? Why am I not praying over and over again, begging and pleading God for answers to my prayers? Why don't I pray with expectation that He will answer?

It is never **one-and-done** with God. Yes, we have been saved by grace, but at the same time we are to continue to **"work out our salvation"**. This includes interceding for others and for ourselves. We are called to be relentless prayer warriors. We need to show God that we know we are in desperate need of Him.

Father God,

Help me to have faith like this widow. Help me to not give up. Help me to have faith that you care and want to hear my requests, even my repentance. Help me to never stop believing and hoping in you! Help me to be confident that you will answer my prayers. Thank you for being God and I am not! Help me to remember and reflect that attitude every day!

In Your Precious Name, I pray,

Amen.

CHAPTER SIXTEEN

Witness

"You may be the only Jesus that someone will ever see." I know this is as true here in prison as it is out there in the world. But it saddens me, nevertheless. I am reminded of this truth every day. Just in the last month the last fight we had in our unit was between two Christians over a television station. One of the men was very outspoken and bragged about his master's degree he had received in "Bible". This week as cellmates begin to change and people move another Christian man was also very outspoken about his faith, and yet refused to give back another man's cell. This caused twelve other people to not be able to return to the cells that were theirs before the pandemic. This issue created all kinds of drama and fights. In another lengthy conversation this week with my cellmate of the Muslim faith, he was quick to point out all the conflicts he's observed in our unit which is supposed to be made up of men of religious faith. He claimed that most of the fights, arguments and cheating come from guys claiming to be Christians. He continued to say, and I had to agree, that some of the most obnoxious and offensive individuals, and the ones addicted to pornography are Christians.

Honestly, this breaks my heart to see how we disgrace the Christian faith. I couldn't help thinking, **no wonder Christians aren't trusted and are often called hypocrites**. It grieves me to the core. As I learn about the other religions, I realize that Christianity has the most to offer its believers. To me, it's an easy choice. God is a loving God who offers us freedom, even inside these walls. God offers us unconditional forgiveness of everything we have ever done or said, no matter how terrible. God gave us His son, to be the ransom for our sin. A blameless man, God's Son, came to Earth for the sole purpose of living and dying for you and me. No other religion has that to offer. There is nothing I must do to be *saved* except believe in Jesus as my Savior. There aren't five certain prayers to say a day. There isn't an act of my will that gives me eternal life. This gift is given to me by grace alone. It really is that simple and it's offered to everyone all of the time.

Yet, we drag Christ's name and His love, and His message through trash when we profess our faith by our mouths and then don't act in a way that honors Him. It is so painful to watch. I wonder what I can do to make that change?

I realize that I can be the change. I can make sure that what I do and say reflects God's love. I can admit when I fall short and make mistakes. I can apologize to the person I have offended. I can forgive those who have offended me. Then, if they'll listen, I can share His message.

> *Father God,*
>
> *Help me to mirror your love, your grace, your mercy, and your forgiveness. When someone in this place sees me, help them to see you through me.*
>
> *In Jesus' Name,*
>
> *Amen.*

CHAPTER SEVENTEEN

Mercy of a Stranger

"Love the Lord your God with all your soul, strength, and mind and love your neighbor as yourself." Who is my neighbor?

My Scripture reading today was out of Luke 10:25-37. It is called the story of "The Good Samaritan". This is a story about a man traveling from one town to another who was attacked, stripped of his clothing, beaten, robbed and left in the ditch. The story describes how the first man to pass by him was a religious leader. He even crossed the street to the other side when he saw the suffering man. Another man also passed him by. Finally, a foreigner, (known as an outcast due to his nationality) was traveling on the road and saw the beaten man. The "foreigner, outcast" dismounted his donkey and cared for the suffering man. He put him on his donkey and took him to the nearest inn where he treated his wounds and paid for the man's lodging and care. Jesus told this story to a religious leader who was trying to trick him.

Many of us are taught to "take care of our own". We look after our own family, maybe our close neighbors and friends, but we might not concern ourselves with those outside of our circle. That idea is exactly opposite of what God is teaching us in this Scripture story.

My first beating was in beating in Miami, after my trial in the prison there where I was waiting to be transferred to this prison. A man beat me up because he wanted my cell. He thought I was delaying the process of him moving into it. Of course, I had no control over it. After he beat me, leaving me with a black eye, busted lip, missing tooth, I followed the "inmate code" and hid out in my cell. I didn't report it and hid from the officers so I wouldn't be noticed. However, word got out and a group of Honduran inmates came to my rescue. They brought me ice, bandages, medical cream and encouragement. They learned who was responsible and proceeded to repay the damages. I didn't ask for any attention or help. I planned to quietly ride it out. Yet, a man of a different race, different culture, different language came to my aid and cared of me, protected me.

They went out of their way to show kindness to a stranger.

It doesn't matter if you are assaulted or in a fight whether it is you to blame, or you're just a victim of a random attack. To show mercy is not based on the merit of whether the person deserves it or not. Mercy is an act of kindness or compassion in order to help another without expecting anything in return. I am surrounded by hundreds of men every day in dire need of mercy. It is up to me to decide whether or not I will offer them mercy. Here's a recent example: A man got into a fight over a television station. To not bring attention to himself, I decided to show him mercy by offering him a bag of ice for his black eye, some make-up to conceal the bruise and some Ibuprofen.

What does *showing mercy* look like for you? How can you show mercy to a stranger?

> *Father God,*
>
> *I pray you will allow me to show mercy to the men I am surrounded by today. Help me to see them as broken and hurting and in need of your love and healing touch. Help me to be willing to offer that today.*
>
> *In Jesus' Name,*
>
> *Amen*

CHAPTER EIGHTEEN

Master or Slave

"Do you not know that when you give yourselves over to someone you become that person's slave? If you are slaves to sin, then you will die. But, if you are slaves who obey God, then you will live a godly life. " (Romans 6:16)

As a teenager, I remember all I wanted to do was to drive. It couldn't happen fast enough for me. I got my permit at age 15 and bought a Honda Spree 50cc moped. I began driving other friend's cars before I received my license. When I was finally able to buy my first car on my 16th birthday, a Nissan Sentra, I was pulled over by the police all on the day I received my license. I tell you this story because this was the first lesson that I taught myself. I bought my own car, paid for my own insurance, now almost had to pay for a ticket, and learned that the day you drive, is the day you become a slave to a job so that you can work to pay to drive. From that day on, I've always had to work, it wasn't a choice.

I wonder what things control you or me? Before I was incarcerated, I had several T.V. shows that I would schedule my free time around. I considered it my "me time". I didn't realize how much control the desire for my "me time" had on my life. Sometimes, as Christians, we see things as "black and white". Maybe we list drinking alcohol as a sin, or dancing as a sin, the list goes on and on depending on perspectives. We need to step back and ask if the action in question, has control over me, or do I have control over it.

As I endured the three-week trial that lasted all day, every day of the work week, the stress and anxiety was almost unbearable. In the evening my loving wife would make me a cup of ice cream topped with Bailey's Irish Cream. That treat, and a hot bath was the only thing that helped me to unwind and be able to get some sleep those weeks.

As I look back, I realize that it was the stress and anxiety that were controlling me more than the need for ice cream-alcohol treat or hot bath. Other questions to ask when trying to determine what is controlling you are: how is it affecting your body, your temple? Is it causing you harm? How is it affecting those you care about? You see, for me, my T.V. shows took my time away from my family time. I was already working 10-12 hours away from home a day. The added two hours of "me time", hurt my family.

Here in prison, Christianity looks quite different than it does on the outside. You see, I don't struggle to find time for prayer and Scripture reading. The temptations here are much different, much less. We don't have access to the "drugs" that are available on the outside. Anything we could get like that is more expensive and more dangerous, less "pure". For example, cigarettes in prison consist of already chewed tobacco from officers that has been dried out and rolled. So disgusting. Many Christians in prison spend hours studying the Bible to complete correspondence Bible Courses. I would say in many cases it is often easier to live like a Christian inside these walls than it is outside. Men still struggle with purity issues behind these walls, but it is milder than the temptations readily available outside. Pornography has been removed from prisons for many years. There might be some suggestive pictures some have found or copied black and whites, but that is rare.

For me, today is a good reminder to stop and evaluate what takes up my time, my thoughts. Reflecting on the verse from Romans causes me to consider what is controlling me and what I control.

> *Father God,*
>
> *I pray that only things that honor you will control my words and actions today. I pray they will be pleasing to you. Help me not to be distracted by the temptations of the world and to focus on you only.*
>
> *In Jesus' Name,*
>
> *Amen*

CHAPTER NINETEEN

Idols

For most of my life I considered idols as things I held in higher importance than my God. Items that I worshipped. I was challenged to look at what I spend the most time doing. I analyzed where I spent most of my money. I considered what occupied my thoughts most of the time. I still believe that all of that falls into "idol worship", but I'm realizing that there are also "real idols" that exist and people worship.

I was exposed to idol worship quite a bit in Haiti. However, it was far removed from my influence. I didn't experience it first-hand as those I associated with believed in honoring God. I often heard about or saw from a distance "idol worship".

But, now in the USP Terre Haute, (prison), I'm in a "religious program unit" where all the participants have to profess a commitment to a religious belief. The men in this unit consist of: Atheists, Pagans, Buddhists, Jewish, Muslims, Christians, Catholics, Agnostics, just to name a few. Many of these religious beliefs come with idol worship.

I see it all around me and I interact with these men on a daily basis. For some it is a bone, to others a blade of grass, and to another a seed. Some have sculpted a statue from clay and others have assembled a statue from random items they'd collected over the years. To others, it's a picture of their god or goddess. Some burn incense in their cells. Some have decorative cloths. Others have made candles.

This morning as I read in Acts 17: 15-34 during my devotional time, my thoughts were drawn to these people, these items, and the acts of worship. I think we're all created to have a need for a "higher power". Many people have a need for god to be something physical. Something they can touch, pray to and use as a symbol for their adoration and love.

Even for many of us Christians, we create private sacred places and altars for us to pray as well. Many of us pray holding a tactile object or kneel before our altar, table, or crucifix. There is nothing wrong with these added objects, but the problem comes when that object becomes what we worship. If it changes from a reminder, or a tool to help us get close to the sacred, to what we worship.

"You should have no other gods before Me, says the Lord." The Bible also refers to God as a "jealous God". God wants to be the first priority in our lives. I have learned that God is not a pompous God, or an arrogant God who wants or demands our worship. God is a loving God who wants what is best for us. It is best for us to keep our priorities in line and to do that God must be first. I've seen that when I focus my time in prayer and Scripture study, my actions and words reflect Christ. God blesses me in my attitude, in my accomplishments and even my direct family and friends are blessed as well.

It's easy to look back and have regrets. I used to work ten to twelve hours a day and I'd come home feeling entitled to some "me time". I would retreat to a warm bath or to watch a television show on my own in my room. Now that I reflect back, I realize my priorities were so out of line. I regret not spending more time with my Lord and my family. I missed out on many valuable hours I could have spent with them because I wasted that time on my "idols".

Don't live with regret. I encourage you not to either. Make the change now. Recognize the things in your life that are keeping you away and distracting you from what is most important.

Father God,

Help me to always put you first in my life. Let my life trickle down your grace, your love, and your mercy that I receive anew every morning. Help me to be an example to others of appreciating what is important.

In Jesus' Name,

Amen

On the following pages are paintings by Danny while in the prison. Being able to go to the Craft Room and work with paints, canvas and leather was a source of peace and creativity for him. Some of these paintings are still available for purchase and others have been purchased with all the proceeds going to the support of the Pye family.

INSPIRATION FROM INSIDE • 73

Danny's Paintings

74 • DANIEL PYE

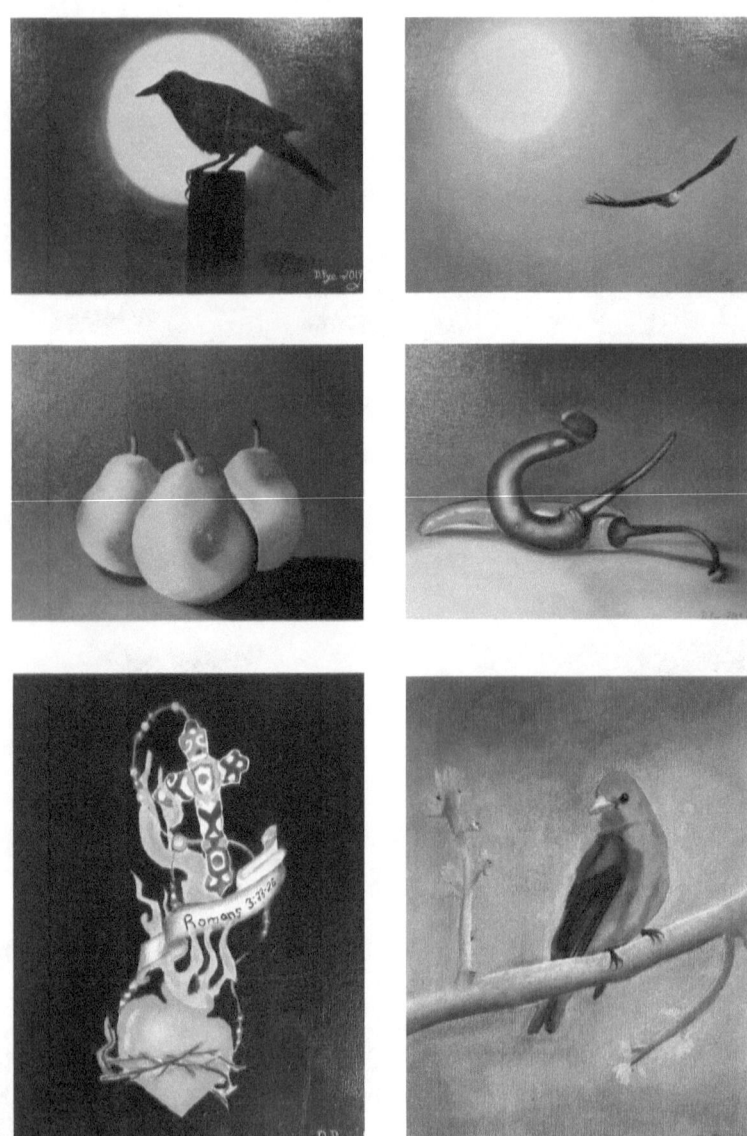

INSPIRATION FROM INSIDE • 75

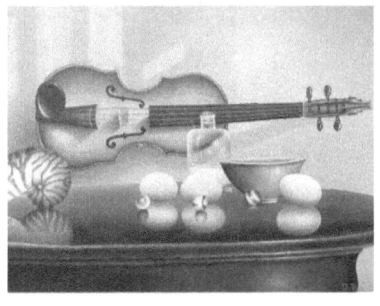

CHAPTER TWENTY

Account

For the past two months, due to the Covid Pandemic, I have had a new "*cellie*". He is a devout Muslim. We have shared hours of conversation about our beliefs. I have spent hours reading from the Bible and he has spent hours reading from the Koran. It has been a time of education and enlightenment. Even though, we haven't converted each other, we have each gained a new respect and understanding for each other and for our different faiths.

We spent Christmas together "locked down" in our cell. I came to see that this was a gift. To share the meaning of Christmas with someone who didn't celebrate it.

One thing he shared with me that I found surprisingly different in our faiths. Upon death, a Muslim believes he is judged by God, which is similar to our Christian belief. However, it differs quite a bit after the judgement. For a Muslim: everyone you have ever encountered is present at your judgement. Each gives a report to God of how you as an individual behaved. Everyone states their case on how you treated them. From these reports, God, "Allah", judges you for eternity. Of course, ultimately, it's God's final decision, but it is based on their testimonies.

"God's grace has saved you because of your faith in Christ. Your salvation doesn't come from anything you do. It is God's gift. It is not based on anything you have done. No one can brag about earning it." Ephesians 2:8-9

I'm not sure about you, but the thought of others that I've had contact with testifying about me is a scary thought. I wonder if those that testify on the good that I've done, would outweigh those that had complaints. It sure is a humbling thought.

God does know everything, so nothing would be a surprise. However, I believe Jesus took all of my past, present and future with Him to the cross when He died for my sins. Will we be held accountable for what we have done or not done? I do believe we will. I believe many suffer the consequences for their sins in this life as well as in the next.

Yet, in Romans 8, Paul states that " neither trouble, or hard times, or harm or hunger, nakedness or danger of war, death or life, or angels or demons, present or future , or any power can separate us from God's love. This verse and the one above about God's grace, gives me hope and relief. I know I wouldn't "measure up" on my own.

> *Father God,*
>
> *Thank you for your grace. Thank you for your salvation. Thank you for taking all of my sins, and all of the times I fell short upon the cross and forgiving me. Thank you that it is no longer up to me, but because of you that I am saved, redeemed and promised eternity with you.*
>
> *In Jesus' Name,*
>
> *Amen*

CHAPTER TWENTY-ONE

Question

Gideon (speaking to an angel): "If the Lord is with us, why has all of this happened to us?" Judges 6:13

Job: "Though I cry, 'violence!' I get no response; though I call for help, there is no justice." Job 19:7

Psalmist: "Awake Lord! Why do you sleep? Rouse yourself!" Psalm 44:23

Ecclesiastes: "Utterly meaningless! Everything is meaningless." Ecclesiastes 1:2

Isaiah: "Truly you are a God who has been hiding himself." Isaiah 45:15

Jeremiah: "Why are you like a man taken by surprise, like a warrior powerless to save?" Jeremiah 14:9

Jesus: "My God, my God, why have you forsaken me?" Matthew 27:46]

Is it ok to question God? Is it ok to wonder why? Many Christians would argue that it isn't right to question God. Many would say it is disrespectful. The fact is, God is all knowing, all powerful, just, perfect, flawless and love.

The fact is, I am not. Neither are you. We don't understand God's reasons or choices. We don't understand why the innocent are allowed to suffer and die. We don't understand why God allows evil to succeed. It seems natural to question and wonder why.

I believe that God is big enough to take our whys and to handle our questions. The above examples are godly men, faithful men, even Jesus himself who questioned. I believe God loves us so much that He wants us to ask why. He wants us to bring our pain and sorrow and confusion to Him. Furthermore, I believe God wants to comfort us in our pain and to rely on Him alone. God doesn't always answer our question of *why*, but He does tell us and show us that He is enough.

I recently read a great book that inspired me to write this blog. I highly recommend it: ***The Question that Never Goes Away,***

Why? by Phillip Yancey. It has greatly helped me in my faith walk.

Too often in the past, when things went wrong, I'd get angry and bitter. I'd stew about it and be filled with unforgiveness. This leads me to my familiar place of despair and depression. Then, I'd search for the reason "Why"?

But now, I'm much healthier, (at least today). When I start to wonder why, I also wonder: "why not"? They go hand in hand. I wonder if I'd be in this place learning to accept His love and be content behind these walls without the many whys in my life.

Father God,

Help me to rely solely on you. Help me to rest in you. Help me to accept what I don't understand and forgive and love through the pain. Help me to find hope where it seems to be absent. Thank you, God for your care and love for me.

In Jesus' Name,

Amen.

CHAPTER TWENTY-TWO

Busy

"Jesus and his disciples went on their way. Jesus came to a village where a woman named Martha lived. She welcomed him into her home. She had a sister named Mary. Mary sat at the Lord's feet listening to what he said, But Martha was busy with all the things that had to be done. She came to Jesus and said, "Lord, my sister has left me to do the work by myself. Don't you care? Tell her to help me!" "Martha, Martha, the Lord answered. You are worried and upset about many things. But few things are needed. Really only one thing is needed. Mary has chosen what is better. And it will not be taken away from her." Luke 10:38-42

As I read this Scripture today, it hits home to me. I wonder if any can relate as well? Too often in my life I choose what is good and I miss out on what is better. Too often I keep myself so busy doing good things, and I miss out on what is best for me.

I can relate to Martha when she cries out to Jesus as she questions Him. Asking if He cares? I have asked God that same thing many times in my life. I wonder if He sees me, if He cares about all I am doing and all that I am giving? I'm learning that is the first sign that I am too busy doing what I think is good and missing out on what is best for my life.

Behind these walls you have endless time to think and reflect. I remember the good and the bad. As I reflect today, I begin to see all the times in my own life, in my ministry of over a decade, that I busied myself with what seemed to be "good works." Sometimes I missed out what would have been "best".

Very few times did I recognize the importance of being still. It took this incarceration for me to learn to stop, slow down, and be still and to listen for that quiet voice. "Be still and know that I am God," (Psalm 46:10)

Too often I got caught in working out my salvation. Too often I was looking for the next big event, next big outreach. I thought that was how God worked. I thought to be successful in His kingdom meant to do something big. To be of excellence, the result had to be huge and visible I believed. Yet, today, I'm reminded that when God spoke to one of His most loved prophets, Elijah, He didn't speak through the powerful wind, or the earthquake, or fire, but in a still, quiet whisper. That's how God choose to reveal Himself and His will to Elijah.

He often still chooses to reveal Himself today in very still, quiet subtle ways. (reference found in 1 Kings 19:11-13)

So, the question I have today for myself first and then to you the reader is, "Are you taking the time to be still and to listen?" "Are you settling for what is good and missing what is better for your life?" It is often easier to settle for what is good and then miss God's perfect plan.

> *Father God,*
>
> *Help me to never settle for what is good. Help me to press on to know your best for me. Teach me to be still and to listen to your whisper in my life. Help me to listen and not just to do!*
>
> *In Jesus' Name,*
>
> *Amen*

CHAPTER TWENTY-THREE

Still

"We fight against this very concept today. Too much of my year has been locked in a 12' x 8'cell being still. Our kids have been locked indoors due to COVID and the weather. The last thing they want to hear is be still. We have sheltered in place for so long and we grow weary of being still.

Yet today I challenge you to thank God for the conditions that are requiring you to be still. Do not ruin these quiet hours by wishing them away, waiting impatiently to be active again. Some of the greatest works in His kingdom have been done from sick beds and prison cells. Some of the most inspiring texts of the New Testament were written by men in chains. Instead of resenting the limitations of a weakened body, limitations of stay-at-home restrictions, search for the will of our

Father in the midst of these very circumstances. Limitations can be liberating when your strongest desire is to live close to our Lord, Jesus Christ.

When I am quiet, when I am still, it only enhances my understanding of His presence, of His love, and of His grace. Do not despise these times. Although you feel cut off from the activity of the world, you might be exactly where God wants you to be. As Paul said, His strength and power show themselves most effective in our weaknesses.

Paul illustrates this for us perfectly in 2 Corinthians 12:7-9: *"God has shown me amazing and wonderful things. People should not think more of me because of it. So I wouldn't become proud of myself, I was given a problem. This problem caused pain in my body. It is a messenger from Satan to make me suffer. Three times I begged the Lord to take it away from me. But he said to me, 'My grace is all you need. My power is strongest when you are weak.' So I am very happy to brag about how weak I am. Then Christ's power can rest on me."*

So today instead of feeling trapped, instead of feeling restricted, instead of despising the locked doors, I will try to see them as an opportunity, an opportunity to be still and listen for God's quiet voice. I will try to see all He has done and all He is still doing. It is not natural or easy, but it replaces my despair with thanksgiving. It replaces my anger with excitement. It replaces my lack of understanding with hope for what is happening to me and for me in the moment and in my stillness.

Today I will choose—***"Be still and know that I am God."*** (Psalm 46:10)

For me, the expression ***the grass is always greener on the other side*** applies. When my cell door is open all day, I want some peace and quiet. I want to crawl in my bunk and shut out all the drama, all the violence, and all the nonsense. I want the door locked. But when the door is locked all I can think about is being out to make a phone call to talk with that family member or friend or check my email. I struggle with finding contentment where I am in the here and now.

Father God,

Help me to be still. Help me to slow down and hear your voice and your guidance. Help me to be content with where you have me right now. Help me not to want more or something different. Thank you for your love.

In Jesus' Name,

Amen

CHAPTER TWENTY-FOUR

With Me

"The Lord is my shepherd. He gives me everything I need. He lets me lie down in field of green grass. He leads me beside quiet waters. He gives me new strength. He guides me in the right paths for the honor of His name. Even though I walk through the darkest valley, I will not be afraid, because You are with me. Your shepherd's rod and staff comfort me. You prepare a feast for me right in front of my enemies. You pour oil on my head. My cup runs over. I am sure that your goodness and love will follow me all the days of my life, and I will live in the house of the Lord forever". Psalm 23

I chose to study this very popular Scripture today and break it down to see how it speaks to me in this modern world and in my circumstances. It begins with words of reassurance: "The

Lord is my shepherd, I shall not want," and paints a word picture of "green pastures and still waters." Then, in contrast, the tone changes as the Psalmist writes "in the presence of my enemies, and in the valley of the shadow of death." In the beginning of the Psalm, God seems distant. The words are about God and what God is doing. Eventually, there is a shift and the Psalmist writes to God: "I will fear no evil because You are with me." God has come close.

Those few words: "You are with me", reveal to me the one thing that I can count on when the world around me feels like it is crumbling down. God is with me! In the midst of COVID-19 scares of new variants, political unrest, the latest natural disaster, whatever it is that scares me: I know that God is with me! No matter our circumstances, we have assurance of "Immanuel" (common name for God that means—*God with us).*

Too often I beg God to take me out of here, to remove me from my distress, from this oppressive environment. I cry out for redemption and salvation. Yet, all of the time, God prefers to work within me and alongside of me in the midst of my trial and hardships.

The best example of this and the biggest proof that God is with us is that God joined creation by sending us Jesus to live among us, no longer as God, but as man. He became one of us. Immanuel. He joined our race. In some of the most dangerous times in Israel, civil war was raging, "The virgin will conceive and give birth to a son and will call him Immanuel." This prophecy from Isaiah came to be. Isaiah called Him: Wonderful Counselor, Mighty God, Everlasting Father, Prince of Peace." This is the same child, the same God who will someday restore justice to all the earth.

So, when I question, where is God? When I plead to be removed from my circumstances, I can know with all confidence that God is with me. Even at times when I feel alone, I know that in fact: He is still with me. *Always!* In my joy and in my sadness, in my anger and in my fear: God is with me. I can't hide from Him. He loves me so much that He is committed to never leaving me or ever forsaking me. No matter what.

> *Father God,*
>
> *Thank you for being Immanuel. Thank you for being with me in my darkest hour. I know you are near. Thank you for never leaving me. Thank you for sharing your love, that while I was still a sinner, you sent Jesus to be born to live and to die to remove my sins and offer me eternal life.*
>
> *In Jesus' Name,*
>
> *Amen*

CHAPTER TWENTY-FIVE

Pride

"Pride comes before a fall."

The expression is true. I see it play out in my own life, in the life of many and in Scripture. As a young adult, I helped reroof a friend's home. I had no idea what I was doing as I had never done that kind of job before. He had roofed before, so I followed his lead. As I do now, I did then, I enjoyed cracking jokes and having fun. As we rolled out the tarpaper over the vents and skylight of his Florida home, I suggested that we mark the holes we just covered. He ignored my suggestion. Hours later, my friend fell in one of the vent holes to his ankle and hurt himself. Of course, my reaction was to laugh and cut up and point out that maybe we should have marked the holes. So that's what we did. The next day, as I was carrying a 70lb. tar bucket across the roof, I fell into one of the marked holes. It was the skylight hole and my hole leg went through. I wonder if I mocked my friend a little less, if I would have injured myself? That sure showed me that pride comes before a fall literally!

Today, as I read 2 Kings, chapter 5, I'm reminded of this lesson as I see how a warrior who was very important to the king of that area handled a chance to be healed by humbling himself. The warrior was given permission by the king to go and see the prophet in Israel who was known to heal people. The servant of the prophet greeted the warrior and gave him the instructions from the prophet to bathe himself in the Jordan river seven times in order to be healed. The warrior was filled with anger when he heard the instructions. He was upset that the prophet himself didn't take the time to greet him as he thought he was an important person and should have seen the prophet directly. He also wondered why the prophet didn't just pray over him personally to heal him. He also was disgusted at the idea of bathing in the dirty Jordan river. He left angry. Fortunately, this warrior had his own servants with him that talked him into following the prophet's instructions. The warrior did so and was healed. His pride almost caused him to miss his chance for healing. His obedience not only healed his body but saved his soul.

What are our obstacles caused by our own pride? In another Scripture in the book of Matthew, chapter 19, verse 20, Jesus tells of a rich man who was asking how to be saved. When Jesus told him to sell all he had and give to the poor and follow Him, the rich man went away sad. His pride wouldn't allow him to do what Christ asked. He missed out on his redemption.

I see it every day in here—incarcerated men who won't let down their pride to follow Christ. They don't understand that letting go of your pride doesn't mean you'll miss out, in fact it means you'll gain everything. By letting go of the here and now, we inherit so much more. Are you willing to humble yourself?

Father God,

Make me into a humble servant. Help me to not hold tight to false identity, false wealth, false security of this world. Help me to humble myself to live for you and to serve you and to point others to do the same.

In Jesus' name,

Amen

CHAPTER TWENTY-SIX

The Fall

It 's easy. You can take it anywhere, and you already take it everywhere. It's only one click away. It's free. It's sensual. It's fun. You can even delete your history. No one will ever know. You are all alone. Just you and your device. But the consequences are eternal. They can be deadly. They can lead to life of emptiness and despair. They can lead to a life of loneliness.

I hear the same thing almost every day. It's just told from a different voice or perspective. It's just one compromise, or one simple excuse. Just one good reason. No one is looking. No one will ever know. I deserve it. Everyone does it. It really doesn't matter.

But those are all lies. Sin traps you. Men become addicts to their substance of sin. That is why prisons are full. It is never just once. One lie leads to another and then another. Before you know it, you don't even know the truth from the lies yourself.

The next lie you believe is that you have to do it to survive. Or you believe that you'll never be caught. It may start as a small sin, but it grows into a larger offense.

"So be careful when you think you are standing firm, you might fall. You are tempted in the same way all other human beings ae tempted. Yet, God is faithful. He will not let you be tempted anymore then you can take. But, when you are tempted, God will give you a way out. Then you will be able to deal with it." 1 Corinthians 10: 12-13

Many of the people here in prison are like those that are free on the street. The only difference is that these people in prison have been caught and convicted of the crime, the sin, that they committed.

It's easy to fall. It's natural to fall. We all in fact fall. However, there are many things we can insert into our lives to protect ourselves from the temptation of falling. First is to know yourself. Know your weaknesses and your strengths. Know where you are most susceptible to falling. Then, guard yourself. Eliminate things or places, events or people that will be stumbling block for you. Replace those things, events, people with others that will be helpful for you to grow into a stronger, better person.

For myself, and for many of the men I am surrounded by in here, we find meeting on a regular basis to be helpful. We pray and study God's word together. We "pull up" one another when we hear or see an action or thought that doesn't align with God's guidelines. We hold each other accountable. God promises us a "way out" when we are tempted or when we fall. So, cry out to Him to provide your way out.

Father God,

I have sinned and fallen short each and every day. Forgive me and help me to create boundaries in my live that will help me to avoid sin, and temptations. But Lord, when I am tempted, help me to run straight to you for the way out. Thank you Lord for your grace and forgiveness. Thank you for providing the way!

In Jesus' Name,

Amen

CHAPTER TWENTY-SEVEN

Understand

How often, when we were children, did our parents or teachers give us instructions that we failed to understand? Sometimes we'd rebel because we didn't agree with them. Even as adults, what may make sense to me, might not be as clear to another. We each approach problems or challenges with different ideas of how to handle them. Just because sometimes someone does it differently than me, doesn't make them wrong. If they're more experienced, or in authority, I may just need to comply with their directions, even if I don't understand their reasoning.

In the book of John, chapter 11, we read the story of Jesus and his friend Lazarus. We know that Jesus loved Lazarus, but at first, we don't understand, just as his sisters didn't understand, why Jesus didn't come immediately when he heard that Lazarus was so sick. In my limited human understanding, it seems that Jesus could have spared his friends a lot of pain if we would've healed him then. There would not have been all of the tears, heartache and mourning at his graveside. However, the fact is that Jesus performed an even greater miracle that was only possible because of Lazarus's death and burial.

In the same way, Jesus still loves His children today. He loves you and me. Just because we may be going through a difficult trial, doesn't mean that He has forgotten us or abandoned us. He still weeps with us today when we suffer, just as He did for Lazarus. He still longs to comfort us in our loss and pain.

Maybe you are experiencing a great loss. One that you can't understand. Jesus doesn't expect you to understand it. He only asks you to wait on Him, to trust in Him, and to obey Him. Someday, He will make it clear. Maybe it won't be here on this earth. Regardless, we need to keep the faith and believe even though it doesn't make any sense. We can have some comfort in knowing that He does understand our pain and suffering.

Why do bad things happen to good people? Why do children suffer and die? Why are innocent men and women imprisoned, tortured, raped or killed? Why is there so much evil in this world? Why are things so unfair? Why do good things happen to bad people? Why do those that serve Christ so faithfully often suffer so unjustly?

Jesus used the resurrection of Lazarus to demonstrate that He is the resurrection and the life. He came into this world to redeem us from sin and death, and to give us life that will never end. Even though sometimes we don't understand, even though it often doesn't make sense, we can be confident in His love for us. We can believe that He wants the best for us.

Too often, I don't understand. Too often correctional officers do things and say things just to be mean. I wonder why? I ask God to help me understand. Sometimes, He helps me with insight, other times I just don't get it. So, I cling to the hope and knowledge that I have in His redemptive love and grace!

Father God,

I do not understand your plan for me. I don't understand the why, how, where and when. God, I know you love me. Help that to be enough for me today.

In Jesus' Name,

Amen

Chapter Twenty-Eight

Purpose

"The son of man came for the lost and to save them."

(Luke 19:10)

During these uncertain times, so many have lost their jobs and some even their homes. So many are in search of their purpose. When you have felt like you've had a purpose for so long and then it's gone, you can feel lost. Often, our purpose defines us. It gives us hope and fulfillment.

I too was wrapped up in my purpose. I was a husband, father, successful manager working 60 plus hours at the hospital. I was helping people. I was making a difference. I was making a good living and was supporting my family. In an instant, like many people can now relate to, it was gone. For me, the cause was very different, but the effects are very similar.

Like so many, I have to re-learn my purpose. I have to find my meaning. For me, this has been a humbling process. It has caused me to realize that I was vain. I lived in the present and didn't look towards the future and what's really important.

Today, I am learning to wake up every day and ask God for His grace to do what He has called me to do. I used to think to have purpose, I had to do something significant. Something that others would respect. I wanted to be recognized, liked and appreciated. I was like the one referred to in the Bible, "The first shall be last and the last shall be first." I never wanted to be last. I wanted to be first, I paid the price, my family paid the price, my friends paid the price, and my Lord paid the price. They all paid the price for my arrogance. I'm still learning this attitude of humility. I am learning how to suffer quietly, without complaining or glorifying myself. I am learning to find meaning and purpose in everything God brings my way and to use that opportunity for His glory and honor.

We all are given unique opportunities to serve God. I too, in prison, as a **born-again** Christian, have great opportunities to serve my Lord. The question is, am I going to use that opportunity or squander it away? Will I complain because this is not the way I want to serve Him? Or will I embrace it?

I am surrounded by men I would not have associated with on my own accord. I am surrounded by men that society has disregarded. Many of them, have been disowned by their families.

They have made some terrible mistakes and done awful things. Yet, I have the unique opportunity to show them Christ's love through my actions and words. I can offer them forgiveness through Christ. I can help them to know His love, acceptance, security and blessings. Yes, even inside these walls.

I have a unique opportunity to continue to parent my children and love my wife, even from a far. I can share with them what God is teaching me. I can teach them about His grace and forgiveness-how to give and how to receive His love. These lessons are more important than what I taught then when I was present.

> *Father God,*
>
> *Help me to listen. Help me to hear. Help me to live your purpose for me each and every day. Help me to be the change that is needed here. Help me to show your love and grace to the men who need it.*
>
> *In Jesus' Name,*
>
> *Amen.*

CHAPTER TWENTY-NINE

Recycled

Growing up as child in central Florida, my family wasn't poor, but we weren't rich either. One of my favorite pass times was to collect aluminum cans for recycling. It was my first source of income as a child, besides my allowance. I really didn't care that I was helping to clean up the environment. I really didn't even understand what recycling meant. All I cared about was the money I could make by doing it.

The same is done by turning old computers, cell phones, or old parts into restored or new gadgets. Despite what the "prosperity gospel" preachers, say, the Bible offers no guarantee that our suffering will be removed from us in this life. The Bible does say that it will be redeemed.

The famous actor, Michael J. Fox is quoted as saying that "learning to live with Parkinson's Disease was the best ten years of my life, not in spite of my illness but because of it." His disease changed everything about who he was and what he could accomplish in his life. He went on to say, "if you were to rush into this room right now and announce that you had struck a deal in which the ten years since my diagnosis could be magically taken away, and traded for ten more years as the person I use to be, I would without a moment's hesitation, tell you to take a hike...I would never want to go back to that life- a sheltered, narrow existence, fueled by fear and livable insulation, isolation and self-indulgence."

We as Christians use an older word: redeem. Our entire faith is based on this simple idea. We see it in many aspects of our lives. Though pain may cause outrage and protest, it also contributes to life. After the fall of Adam and Eve, women have much pain in childbirth. Yet, all is redeemed when the mother holds her precious gift of new life. I witnessed that first hand when my wife bore our three beautiful children. The pain she suffered I couldn't comprehend. However, she never spoke of it as she cared for our children.

Paul told the Romans, "We also glory in our sufferings, because we know that suffering produces perseverance, character, and hope." Paul compared all of his high accomplishments to a pile of dung, yet even that can be recycled as fertilizer.

The crux of our salvation, the execution of God's own son, we refer to as Good Friday. We don't call it dark or tragic. Jesus said himself that he could have called on legions of angels to prevent the crucifixion. He did not. He knew the only way to redemption for mankind was through pain. No way around it. To refine, takes heat, fire. And so it is with us.

Father God,

Thank you for making all things new. Thank you for using all our baggage, all of our hurt, all of our sins and redeeming them for the good of those that love you and are called according to your purpose.

In Jesus' Name,

Amen

CHAPTER THIRTY

Condemned

The purpose of the law is to instruct right from wrong.

The purpose when enforcing the law is to condemn. There is no grace in the law. There is no mercy in the law. You are either guilty of not following the law or you are innocent. Once condemned, once presumed guilty, nothing else matters. It doesn't matter how much you obeyed the laws in the past. All that matters is the one time you didn't. You are condemned for the wrong that you did that one time. You are considered guilty.

Some criticize the law. Some hope for a king to abolish the restrictions. However, the law brings order and peace. We can't have peace and order without the law. Everyone would make their own standards for living. It would be chaotic and unsafe.

Some despise correction and discipline; however, it is necessary for order to prevail.

"My son, do not hate the Lord's training. Do not object when He corrects you. The Lord trains those He loves. He is like a father who trains the son He is pleased with." (Proverbs 3:11-12)

What was Jesus' purpose? What is God's purpose today? Does God support our laws? Does He support our justice system? Does He condemn?

"Do not think I have come to get rid of what is written in the Law or in the prophets. I have not come to do this. Instead, I have come to fulfill what is written." (Matthew 5:17)

We have all sinned. We have all fallen short of God's glory. All of us are condemned for we have all done wrong. Some of the most decent correctional officers are the ones that see us inmates as human beings. They recognize we are individuals with our own good and our own bad. Correctional officers that realize they too have made grievous mistakes and are quick to admit them. It could be that they are using drugs or overindulging in alcohol or have gotten into a fight. They realize that they have similar failings as the inmates. Of course, there are some extreme cases in here. However, many individuals locked up today have been swept away by an addiction that they really need rehabilitation help with overcoming it, not incarceration. They need good counseling, not condemnation. Many need to be shown mercy and grace.

That is where God comes in, because he did not come to condemn, but to fulfill the law. He did this by giving up his son as an innocent atonement to pay the price for our sins. He came to give grace not condemnation.

"Those who belong to Christ Jesus are no longer under God's judgement. Because of what Christ Jesus has done, you are free. You are now controlled by the law of the Holy Spirit who gives you life. The law of the spirit frees you from the law of sin that brings death." (Romans 8:1-2)

So how will you respond to God's gift of grace? Are you quick to pass judgement? Are you quick to condemn? Are you quick to show forgiveness? Are you quick to show grace and mercy?

> *Father God,*
>
> *Help me to be known as a man that shows your love, your grace. Help me not to judge or condemn, but to love the broken and lead them to right living with you.*
>
> *In Jesus' Name,*
>
> *Amen.*

CHAPTER THIRTY-ONE

Compromise

What is the difference between compromise and negotiation?

"Daniel decided not to make himself "unclean" by eating the king's food and drinking his wine. So, he asked the chief official for a favor. He wanted permission not to make himself "unclean' with the king's rich food and wine." (Daniel 1:8)

As you read on in this story you read that Daniel negotiated with the king's official and the king's official compromised with Daniel giving him permission not to eat or drink of the king's food and wine. When we negotiate, we cannot compromise as if we do it leads to sin. Daniel stood strong in his faith.

God showed him much favor because he would not compromise.

"Then Saul said to Samuel, 'I have sinned. I've broken the Lord's command. I haven't done what you directed me to do. I was afraid of the men. So, I did what they said I should do." (1 Samuel 15:24)

We see this over and over again, when leaders compromise what God has called them to do, due to their fear of other men. Because of their desire to please other men they often compromise too. We see this today a lot in politics, in our own leaders making promises that they never keep in order to be voted into office. Too often it is easier to see this in others than it is to see it in ourselves.

I often find it hard to be surrounded by criminals, angry guards and not find myself compromising. For me, it may be in using another person's ID number so that I can make an additional phone call. Or maybe I buy "stolen" vegetables or cheese from kitchen employees. Not matter how you say it, I know it is still compromising my morals and values. It is still a sin, even if minor, to be deceitful or dishonest. When I compromise, it hurts my ability to be a good witness for Christ and it hurts my relationship with my God.

Romans 6:12 says, "So don't let sin rule your body, which is going to die. Don't obey it's evil desires."

And in Romans 14:15, "Your brother or sister may be upset by what you eat. If they are, you are no longer acting as though you love them. So don't destroy them by what you eat. Remember that Christ died for them."

Early in my marriage, my wife who was raised by alcoholics, needed me not to drink or have alcohol in our home. I honored that. I built trust with her, so she soon knew I was not going to be an alcoholic. Today, both my wife and I drink occasionally and have no issue with it. However, to honor her, I'm glad that I didn't compromise and followed through with honoring her request.

In our vows, I promised to give up what I wanted for what we wanted.

"Be careful to obey the rules and laws the Lord gave Moses for Israel. Then you will have success. Be strong and brave. Don't be afraid. Don't lose hope." (1 Chronicles 22:13)

So, what are you tempted to compromise? What compromises do you make that go against your morals? What's an example of a compromise you have refused? Do you see a blessing or a provision because of your obedience? Compromise is essential to make any relationship work long term, but we don't have to compromise what we believe is right.

God, help me to hold steadfast to your law and to your love. Hope me to learn when to compromise and when not to compromise. Help me worry about honoring you with all I do and say.

In Jesus' Name,

Amen

CHAPTER THIRTY-TWO

All

"Then Jesus came to them. He said, 'All authority in heaven and on earth has been given to me. So, you must go and make disciples of all nations. Baptize them in the name of the Father, and of the Son, and of the Holy Spirit. Teach them to obey all things I have commanded you. And you can be sure that I am all ways with you, to the very end.'" (Matthew 28:18-20)

My wife always hated when I would make generalities like, "You always, you never, all the time, you don't, you only..." And she had good reason because when conflict occurred, I often used them carelessly to prove my point. Yet, in the Scripture above we see it used intentionally and repeatedly.

One of the most significant Scriptures, in my opinion, and in my life is the final verse of the gospel of Matthew, known as the **Great Commission**. Jesus passes the baton on to us, his followers. He gives us his instructions, his expectations for what we should do, say, and to whom, and when, and ends with the promise that He will be with us through it all, to the very end.

Absolute authority is never held by any one person. Some may think they are above the law or that they have all of the authority in a matter. We saw that firsthand when our past president of the United States tried many times to exert his authority. He had a lot of authority as president, but still far from absolute authority. Only one holds <u>all</u> authority and He was specific to state that truth in the above verse.

We as human beings are too quick to try to grab authority. We want more and more of it. Many of us have issues with authority. We don't want others to have authority over us. Many people abuse the authority they have been entrusted with and use it to lord over another or to cause harm, to demean, to embarrass others. I struggle with those that micro-manage their authority. I have also struggled in the past with being too trusting and giving too much authority and control away. We sometimes forget that with great authority comes great responsibility.

In the parable of the **Good Samaritan**, Jesus taught us that who our neighbor is has nothing to do with proximity to where we live. In the same way, we are told to go to every nation. We used to think of that as a job for missionaries. That is no longer the case. We have access to almost everyone all over the world at a touch of a button. America is home to people of all nations. We need to reach all nations, yet we don't have to travel to do that anymore. We can do that by simply showing love to all people, no matter their race, culture, or creed.

We have a job as parents, teachers, preachers, bosses, employees and friends. We are to teach all things that God commanded. We are not to leave it up to the Church. The **Great Commission** is for you and me. We should share it by our words and actions. Teach all the commands God has instructed.

The best part is that we are not alone. Surely, God is with us, <u>all</u> ways and in <u>all</u> times.

> *Thank you, God for always being there and for always caring for me. Thank you that you will never leave me or forsake me. Help me to pass that love along to another today.*
>
> *In Jesus' Name,*
>
> *Amen*

CHAPTER THIRTY-THREE

Meant

Have you noticed that what you mean and what the outcome is are often different and even in conflict with each other? I often have the best intentions but then my follow through lacks and I fail. I may mean something one way, but it comes out another way. A simple example is that I meant to work on my "to do list" today, but a friend asked me to play cards.

The famous story in the Bible, in the book of Genesis, of Joseph and his jealous brothers illustrates this issue with "meant". Joseph's brothers were so jealous of him, that they plotted to kill him. The eldest brother persuaded the other brothers to sell Joseph into slavery instead of killing him. God used this horrible situation for His glory and even for Joseph and his family's benefit.

My favorite verse in this story is the words of Joseph to his brothers found in Genesis 50:20, ***"You planned to harm me, but God planned it for good. He planned to do what is now being done. He wanted to save many lives."***

So, not only did Joseph forgive his brothers for their evil deeds, but God redeemed what was meant to be a horrible situation for a better one. I wonder how many times I have missed that lesson in my own life? I have had many who want to bring me harm. How many times has God used that for His glory and honor? The truth is God loves us so much and really wants the best for us, even if we fail to recognize how He is at work in our lives. That is God's heart, His nature.

"I know the plans I have for you announces the Lord: I want you to enjoy success. I do not plan to harm you. I will give you hope for the years to come." (Jeremiah 29:11)

That is the Lord's true intentions for you and me. It's as plain as day, and it's in black and white. Another encouraging Scripture for me is the promise that God gives those of us who know Him.

"We know that in all things God works for the good of those who love Him. He appointed them to be saved in keeping with His purpose." (Romans 8:28)

Too often we have the wrong intentions or wrong motives. God can still use that for His glory and honor. Why are we really going to church? Why are we teaching that Scripture? What is the intent of what we say or do? How do we want to be seen?

Father God,

Open my eyes to your favor for me for my life. Help me to see your steady hand guiding me each step of the way. Help me to be thankful when you turn around the intention of evil for good. Thank you for loving me!

Amen

CHAPTER THIRTY-FOUR

Neglect

Too often we put off what we can for tomorrow, or next week, or for someone else to do. Why do you neglect? What do you put off?

Read Matthew 25:1-30

The Scripture tells us two stories. The first story is of 10 bridesmaids who were out waiting for the arrival of their groom. Five of the women brought their lamps as well as extra oil. The other five didn't bring extra oil. So, when the groom approached the five women without the extra oil panicked and ran to find more oil. They missed out on the groom's arrival, on the wedding feast and celebration.

Jesus tells us this story to remind us to always be ready as we don't know when He will return. Will He find us sleeping? Will He find us unprepared, rushing to finish our responsibilities? We He find us in regret of not urging our brothers and sisters to turn from their evil ways and accept Christ's love and grace? Will we be prepared when our time is up?

The second story is told of a master who goes away for a long time and entrusts his three servants with a different amount of money to manage in his absence. The first servant entrusted with the most money doubles what he was given. The second servant was given less, but still doubles it. The third servant was motivated by fear and hid the money he was given. He returned it just as it was given to him. The master rewarded the first two servants and chastised the third for not even considering to deposit into the bank to make some interest.

We are told this story as a challenge. We need to consider what we are doing with the time we are given. What are we doing with our talents? What are we doing with our resources? What motivates us: fear, success, hope? What will the master find when He returns? How did we use our gifts, our talents, and resources for His kingdom?

I have so many regrets in my own life. I have neglected much in my life. I have put off things I should do many times. Now, I have endless time to reflect and remember. I am learning from my mistakes.

We have been locked down for most of each day due to the Covid 19 pandemic. There is much to do in the little time we are allowed out of our cells. Phone calls, emails all cost a lot. 300 minutes does not go very far in a month. It really makes you prioritize what is important.

My Dad passed away earlier this week. Since my incarceration, he has become my best friend, my biggest advocate. Over the years, but especially these last months, I have called my Dad just to tell him how much I love him. Sometimes, I've even called twice a day. I wanted him to know how proud of him I was for the life he lived and the example he left for me to follow. I had the privilege of speaking with him and telling him how much I loved him and how much he meant to me just before he breathed his last breath. I know he heard me. I don't regret that!

Now, as I talk with my own family, my children, I make sure that I tell them how much I love them and how proud I am of them.

"Don't worry about tomorrow. Tomorrow will worry about itself. Each day has enough trouble of its own." (Matthew 6:34)

> *Father God,*
>
> *Help me to live in the moment. Help me to live in today. Help me to end each day with love and grace and compassion to those you bring into my life.*
>
> *In Jesus' Name,*
>
> *Amen*

CHAPTER THIRTY-FIVE

Exposed

Read Matthew 7:1-20

Millions of people around the world have become sick or have died after being exposed to the coronavirus. So far, myself and my older brother and his family are the only ones I know of who have been sick in our family. For us in prison, if we go on an "outside" trip to the hospital, we are put on quarantine before we can rejoin our unit. The same thing happens if you're transferring in or out of the prison, you are quarantined, first. My teenage daughter volunteers in the nursery at her church. She was recently exposed by another volunteer. This caused her to have to quarantine at home and take her high school classes online for two weeks. Seems like it's affecting everyone, somehow.

How has the virus exposed your attitude or priorities? When fear of this disease caused churches, schools, and businesses to close, and prompted stay at home orders, social distancing and masking in public, we were all exposed. Some people found themselves standing on the side of being cautious due to their fears. Others found themselves standing on the side of misguided faith and didn't worry, maybe were even a bit careless. Some believed it was just a conspiracy. Others feared for their lives. Stress and inconvenience became more common. Parents became teachers. Many learned to work remotely. Most learned to live without family gatherings, parties, recreational activities and sporting events. The list goes on and on.

Yes, we've all been exposed. We have been tempted to despise the leaders of nations, states, churches and schools because of how they're handling this pandemic. We are quick to place blame on those we think allowed or caused this to happen. We wish our lives could go back to "normal".

I remember how angry I got at the exposure of Covid 19 here in the prison. I was angry at the guards that refused to wear masks yet forced us to wear masks. I was angry when there was a breakout of Covid 19 in our unit that caused us to be locked down for a year. No precautions were taken to stop the spread inside. Eventually almost every prisoner became sick. We could no longer have visits. Our time to communicate with family and friends was severely limited.

In Matthew Chapter 7, Jesus gives us several helpful principles for times like this. In verses 1 and 2 He teaches that we should be careful about the way we judge others, for we will be judged in the same way. In verses 3-5 He shows that we need to take care of our own attitudes and problems before we try to help others with theirs. How would I fare if I judged my own heart and motives with the same attitude that I judge others? Verse 12 is the Golden Rule, "Do unto others as you would have them do unto you." Verses 16-20 speak of the fruit of a tree and how it shows whether the tree is good or bad. What has the Corona Virus exposed about the fruit that we bear?

There is no doubt that the Corona Virus has exposed a lot in the past year, both good and bad. It is not too late to right the wrongs. We need to use this time to search and seek out what God has enabled us to change, and we need to change it.

Father God,

Expose the wrong thinking. Expose the harm that I cause others. Expose the things I say or do that does not align with your will. I pray that you will help me to correct what needs to be corrected and to live a life worthy to be called your child.

In Jesus' Name,

Amen

CHAPTER THIRTY-SIX

Overcome

"Don't let evil overcome you. Overcome evil by doing good." (Romans 12:21)

There is an inmate that is my neighbor, in the next cell. He is a little guy, maybe 5 foot. Yet he is very muscular and in good shape. His body is covered in tattoos. He is a new Christian. He tries so hard to stay "clean". He attends every class and completes every assignment. He'd be the first to help someone in need.

As we talk daily, and live side by side, I see him slowly drift back into some of his old behaviors. He was once a gang member. Actually, for most of his life, which was the only life he knew before now. He was exposed to gang activity as a child and it became part of his life at a very young age.

He tries so hard to make positive changes. He surrounds himself with healthy individuals. Yet, as he drifts back to his old lifestyle, he uses the language of before, he carries himself with that style, and starts to associate with others from that background. We call it his "front".

S.I.S. is the name for an internal group of officers that monitor prisoners and investigate when there is suspicious behavior. He was notified this past week about being taken out of the "Faith Life program". He may be sent back to an "active yard". That is a prison that is filled with gang members and is known for violence. SIS is doing this to him because they suspect that he is still corresponding with gang members and is "active." To be at this prison, and in this unit, you cannot be an active gang member.

The catch is that after you have been in this "non-active yard", in this penitentiary you can never be in an "active yard" again. You would be killed instantly. To be allowed to be at this penitentiary and in this yard, you would have had to confess about your gang membership, or even have been given information about your gang to the authorities and be labeled a "snitch". Or you could be placed here as a "sex offender" which is a charge unacceptable to gang members.

To overcome is to conquer, or to make helpless or exhausted according to the Merriam-Webster dictionary.

As I see in my life, and in the life of many others, that we are surrounded by evil. It is impossible to avoid the evil completely. So, how do we overcome it? We overcome evil by doing good. This is so true in overcoming self-centeredness, depression, and an entitled spirit, and much more. It requires to do good.

> *Father God,*
>
> *I pray for your grace and your mercy to help my friend. Please protect him and draw him to you. Help him to overcome his own evil ways. Help me to overcome my own evil ways. Help me to follow you more closely, and to continue to guide other men to do the same.*
>
> *In Your Name, I Pray.*
>
> *Amen*

CHAPTER THIRTY-SEVEN

Preparedness

"So, keep watch. You do not know on what day your Lord will come. You must understand something. Suppose the owner of the house new what time of night the robber was coming. Then, he would have kept watch. He would not have let his house be broken in to. So, you also much be ready. The son of man will come at an hour when you don't expect him." (Matthew 24:42-44)

This Scripture talks about our spiritual state. Which, in the end, is most important. But for me, to better understand the spiritual side, I must relate it to my physical side.

During the Covid pandemic, I was well prepared. One of my ministries in prison is to have helpful medication on hand. I have a small stockpile of almost everything that we can buy at the commissary. As people became sick with Covid, I had something to offer them to relieve their cough, headache, fever and pain. My cellie also helped out by giving away his extra inhalers to help those who were struggling to breathe. I obviously didn't know about the upcoming pandemic when I started saving the medical supplies. God used the fact that I did for those in need. By being prepared, I was able to share Christ's love.

There are countless examples in the Bible of the value of being prepared. One famous passage is about the bride having oil in the lamp for the bride groom on their wedding night. Another is to be prepared to give an answer when asked about your faith.

In this environment, it's easy to see the importance of being prepared. A lock down can happen at any time without notice. It can last a day or up to six months, or even longer if a guard is hurt or killed. After learning that in my first month in here, I started saving supplies.

There is talk among the Christian community these days that Christ is coming soon. They reference the pandemic and political unrest as signs. They may be right. How ready am I? If Christ comes today, have I made sure everyone I love and care about has received the good news? Have I used my time and talents wisely? Have I adequately shared Christ with all I have encountered? For me, the answer to those questions is no. As much as I long to be united with my Lord and Savior in paradise forever, I am still here. I still have more work to do. There is more for me to do to prepare for eternity. My purpose is not yet complete.

A close friend of mine, who spent years inside these walls as a paraplegic was finally pardoned just a week ago. He was incarcerated for 23 years. He was serving a life sentence for a non-violent crime. He recently accepted Christ as his savior and has been growing in his faith. He became a great painter and was able to sell his paintings and saved money. I wonder how prepared he was for life as a free man.

Many people in prison wear their work boots from 5:00 am to 9:30 pm. Others carry what is called a shank or a handmade knife all of the time. These men are prepared to fight at any time.

No one likes to be caught off guard. Life is fragile. Tomorrow is not promised to us. So, I try in all of my interactions to be prepared. I think, if this is the last time I see them, what will they remember from our interaction. Did I let them know how much they meant to me? Did I tell them I loved them? Were my words and actions kind?

We need to be prepared for whatever life brings. More importantly, we need to be prepared for eternity. We need to help others to be prepared before life ends.

Father God,

Help me to always be ready to give a reason for my hope. Help me to be the reason and to show the reason. Help me to always be aware that my words and actions can point others towards faith in you. Thank you for instructing us and preparing us for eternity with you.

In Jesus' Name,

Amen

"Who the Son sets free is free indeed"
(John 8:36)

www.ingramcontent.com/pod-product-compliance
Lightning Source LLC
Chambersburg PA
CBHW022018290426
44109CB00015B/1219